EZ TIMES TABLE

A fun, right-brain approach to learning multiplication and division where kids play with patterns and make friends with numbers

by
Thomas Biesanz
a.k.a. MisterNumbers

September 2008
Growth-Ink Publishing
4025 State Street #9
Santa Barbara, CA 93110
Library of Congress Catalog
Control Number: 2008905174
ISBN 978-0-9799636-1-2
copyright 2008 Thomas Biesanz
Art work by Jakob Marsh
http://EZTimesTable.com

WHAT TEACHERS SAY

"Some of my students who have had trouble memorizing their multiplication and division facts have been lucky enough to work with our school math coach, Tom Biesanz. He has devised a brilliantly simple and easy to use system he calls the **EZ TIMES TABLE** to help the students learn their basic facts. As Tom so aptly puts it, "The students begin to own their numbers" after learning how the system works.

I look forward to learning more about Tom's **EZ TIMES TABLES** myself, so I can incorporate it into my own teaching practice."

-Greg, 5ᵗʰ grade teacher

"Many of the teachers are talking about how the kids are learning with your system and we want to use it next year in our school. The kids seem to enjoy the system and they like discovering this "trick" system. It seems very helpful and useful."

-Laura, 2ⁿᵈ grade teacher

"I am excited about **EZ TIMES TABLE** and its structured, concrete, and logical approach to multiplication and division. Counting by 2's up to 64 becomes the foundation of understanding the more difficult facts. I taught my 22 fourth graders how to build their own EZ TIMES TABLES and their comments reflected their discoveries as the inquiry process helped them see the relationships between numbers and facts. I also presented EZ TIMES TABLES at a faculty meeting and 6 teachers asked for a copy so they too could teach EZ TIMES TABLES to their students."

-Francis, 3ʳᵈ grade teacher

"The EZ TIMES TABLE is a helpful tool for both remediated and excelled math students. Students are able to construct the entire multiplication table using this ingenious format. Number patterns are laid out for discovery. My students enjoyed the success of zipping through the process. I enjoyed looking at the completed table with them and exploring all the extended activities."

-Teresa, 3rd Grade Teacher

WHAT STUDENTS SAY

"I like **EZ TIMES TABLE** because it is fun and cool."   **-Anthony, 3ʳᵈ grade**

"Numbers seemed hard when I first started doing them, but I'm learning all the patterns and tricks and now they are easy."   **-Lylah, 4ᵗʰ grade**

"I like it because it helps me."   **-Enrique, 4ᵗʰ grade**

"Thank you, I always wanted to learn multiplication." (after one 20 minute session)
      -Lauren, 2ⁿᵈ grade

CONTENTS

PART 1: Creating the EZ Times Table (EZTT)

PART 2: Playing with Patterns

PART 3: Advanced Tables with the EZTT

INTRODUCTION

The EZ Times Table creates **a structure,** unavailable elsewhere, that students use **to get a right-brain overview of numbers**. By playing with patterns in math, the student makes friends with numbers while **learning multiplication, as well as addition, subtraction, division, squares, fractions, prime numbers, graphing and tables** revealed in this structure. This Table, with variations, can be useful for learning math in K-5th grade**.**

The overview and the fun patterns, along with sound, rhythm, and focusing on relationships between numbers are the essence of this playful right-brain approach to teaching math. **The EZ Times Table is essentially a graphic organizer.** Students create a table on one page that displays numbers and their relationships viewed both as addition and multiplication. The Table helps students understand multiplying, enhances recall, and gives them an aid in memorizing the times table. It is exciting for students and stimulates their curiosity. Students create their own number lines to 32, and next to that they count by Twos to 64. They are creating important scales of numbers as a foundation.

I used an early version of this method teaching Lauryn. Before learning the EZ Times Table, she cried, **"I can't do math."** Reluctantly, she was willing to count by Ones, and then Twos, using patterns. After a few minutes of **following fun patterns in the other columns, she had finished her Table revealing the multiplication tables that made sense to her.** Two days later I saw that her *EZ Times Table* was on her desk. She said, "I am using my *Table* for all my problems!" Later she said, "Can you laminate it for me?" She now has a positive attitude about math.

This book is for teachers and parents who want to help learners of any age using a right-brain approach to the times table. The first section of the book shows how to create an *EZ Times Table.* The middle section of the book contains ways to put the EZ Times Table to work. The final section reveals EZ variations and the *Rule of Tens* which allows us to create a 20 x 20 times table, and other fun patterns. All a student needs to know to make an EZ Times Table is counting to ten, knowing even numbers, and counting by Fives.

This book grew out of my belief that numbers are fun and easy. Numbers contain patterns and kids of all ages love patterns. Because the student makes the EZ Times Table themselves from simple directions, they value and trust it, and it becomes their anchor for learning and understanding multiplication as repeated addition (3 X 5 is 5 + 5 + 5).

GETTING TO KNOW NUMBERS AS FRIENDS

All families of Numbers (the Ones, Twos, Threes, etc.) are capitalized here because they are names of friends. The Ones and Twos are like family trees that students use to identify the other numbers. All whole numbers are either Odd or Even, just like all students are boys or girls. The Table **separates the Odd and Even columns** so we can look at all the similarities and relationships as well as the differences.

 All columns end in a repeated pattern in the ones-units. For example, the Twos end in 2, 4, 6, 8, 0 and repeats forever (1**0**, 1**2**, 1**4**, 1**6**, 1**8**, 2**0**). The Ones are obvious and the Fours end in 4, 8, 2, 6, 0 (2**0**, 2**4**, 2**8**, 3**2**, 3**6**, 4**0**). Every number has a pattern. See the important **Rule of Tens** on page 56 to see all the patterns and how they relate.

SIMPLE PATTERNS FOR THE EZ TIMES TABLE

 Beyond the 1, 2, 3, 4, 5, 6, 7, 8, 9, 0 pattern of the Ones and the 2, 4, 6, 8, 0 pattern of the Twos, and counting by 5's, we use **simple dot patterns involving sound and rhythm for right-brain learning.** Creating these very simple patterns is **intuitive** for the students and a minimal direction is often sufficient, for example, "Go ahead and do the Eights."

 The second or third time working with a student, the instructions can be shortened. They can sometimes create the whole Table with minimal or no help in a few minutes. Students learn to **re-create all or part of it on graph paper** or scratch paper for **standardized tests,** or anywhere they choose. The **Multiplication Facts Table** replaces the patterns with actual numbers after the basic table is solid and understood. This Table gives the student many anchors in learning the Twos, Threes, Fours, Fives, Sixes, Sevens, Eights, Nines, Tens, and more. The structure allows them to fill in facts that are in doubt: *"5 Fours are 20 so 6 Fours are one more four (20 + 4 = 24) and 7 Fours are two more fours (20 + 4 + 4 = 28)."*

 To initially make the Table, **follow the simple instructions on the top of each left page** and stop at *Additional information*. Each step is illustrated in a Table on the right page. The facts, ideas and suggestions that follow *Additional information* are not necessary to make your Table. Read *"Additional information"* if you want to answer questions, break down steps, to satisfy your curiosity, or for information about teaching.

 Use the illustration of each step on the right-hand pages for clarification. With a student I will point with my pencil tip to tell them where to start each step. I have made the instructions very detailed and clear. I show each step in making the Table. **All Instructions on One Page** are condensed on page 40. Many of the instructions involve repeating patterns and I use **ellipses (...)** to indicate when to continue an established pattern. If you have questions, look at the final Table or contact me at: Tom@eztimestable.com.

 Students often get fascinated by the patterns and find it easy to create the EZ Times Table. Adults, including some teachers, tend to **LOOK** at it and try to understand how it works. Please avoid this temptation. Follow the directions and make one yourself. Copy the blank *EZ Times Table* here or remove the extra one on page 39 (**All Instructions** page is on the back) or use the following instructions with Tables illustrating each step.

EZ Times Table

The EZ Times Table (EZTT) has only ten columns (going down) for the numbers 1-10. The two middle columns, for the Ones and Twos, are gray.

To create the Table, turn to page 8 now.

Additional information: (read on for more facts, ideas, suggestions, etc., but the following is not necessary for making your first Table).

Part of the power of this system is that the students totally create it from an empty table. The left five columns are for odd numbers 1, 3, 5, 7,and 9 (starting at the middle gray column). The right columns are for the even numbers: 2, 4, 6, 8, and 10 (starting with the Twos in the middle). A triple line divides the Even and Odd numbers.

Colored pencils can be used for each number column for definition and aesthetics. It looks great! Most students, however, can use an ordinary pencil and make a clear and meaningful Table.

Notice that four columns are split by dotted lines for two-digit numbers. The far left column and the far right column are split to create the two-digit numbers that makes up the Nines and Tens. The Ones and Twos also have dotted lines splitting the column to emphasize their patterns. The left three columns and the far right column have only ten rows for the Nines, Sevens, Fives and Tens.

This Table is very empowering. Students see that it is empty and they easily create the times table while doing fun patterns. This gives them a sense of mastery and ownership. At the end of a session, I offer students my printed version of the Table and most of them say, *"No, I have MINE!"* They know they created it. It is a great study guide to memorize the times table. **Students have also learned to create the Table on blank or graph paper for standardized tests if they desire.**

Many young students reverse their numbers (when 5 might become ꙅ). On the left of the blank **EZTT,** the cartoon numbers 1-9 can show young students how to make the numbers correctly. The cartoon numbers can also be used to help students define **Odd and Even Numbers** using every other number. The Chart is also a good exercise in writing number sequences because they create all the numbers on the Table.

There is an extra empty table on page 39 to use. Make copies for yourself or a class to make your own EZ Times Table. It also has *All Directions On One Page* on the back.

EZ TIMES TABLE

	Odd Numbers					Even Numbers			

Use the Ones column to multiply the Fives, Sevens, Nines, and Tens.

THE ONES
A step in creating the Ones

To create the Ones column as a pattern:

➢ Put a big 1 above the left gray column.

➢ Write the numbers 1, 2, 3, 4, 5, 6, 7, 8, 9, and 0 going down the right side of the dotted line in the first ten boxes of the left gray column.

➢ Repeat the 1, 2, 3, 4, 5, 6, 7, 8, 9, 0 pattern all the way down the right side of the dotted line, ending at a 2.

Your Table now looks like the one on the right.

To create the Table, turn to page 10 now.

Additional information: for teachers and curious students (read on for more facts, ideas, suggestions, etc. but the following is not necessary for making your first Table).

The student is creating the numbers 1-32 in the left gray column.

Be aware that any errors in the Ones or Twos column throw off the answers. Make sure the last box is 32.

In this pattern method, the two numbers on both sides of the dotted line will create the Ones column. This process is helpful for students because it is more accurate and because it has them thinking in patterns, which is useful in working with numbers.

Even young students know that the Ones are repeating patterns, so it is good for them to put it to use and create this simple number series. They trust the Ones to create 11, 12, 13, ... A first grader or younger can create the Ones column and use it as a number line. Later they can use it to move easily and seamlessly into multiplication. Older students can use this as a review and for building a recognition of patterns that they will use immediately in the Twos column.

The repeating ones-digit pattern for the Ones is 1-2-3-4-5-6-7-8-9-0. We will use this pattern in Part 2 and Part 3 of the book.

EZ TIMES TABLE

		Odd Numbers		1		Even Numbers			
				1					
				2					
				3					
				4					
				5					
				6					
				7					
				8					
				9					
				0					
				1					
				2					
				3					
				4					
				5					
				6					
				7					
				8					
				9					
				0					
				1					
				2					
				3					
				4					
				5					
				6					
				7					
				8					
				9					
				0					
				1					
				2					

Use the Ones column to multiply the Fives, Sevens, Nines, and Tens.

The Ones-A Table ©Thomas Biesanz 2007 www.eztimestable.com

THE ONES
(continued)

➤ Now you can create 10, 20, and 30 by putting 1, 2, and 3 in front of the first, second, and third zeros.

➤ This is followed by writing 1 on the left side of the dotted line between 10 and 20, writing 2 between 20 and 30, and then two 3's to create 31 and 32.

You have created the numbers 1-32 in the boxes.

To create the Table, turn to page 12 now.

Additional information:

This is your Ones column. It should look like the column on the right page. The tens-digits are on the left and the ones-digits are on the right. For example, in the tenth row the 1 is on the left of the dotted line and the 0 is on the right. This creates the number 10. Ending at 32 confirms that no numbers have been missed.

This column reinforces that to multiply any number times one gives the original number. This is a good time to do multiplication problems using 1. It is easy, boosts confidence, and gets the students using the Table. Younger students also use this as a number line for adding and subtracting. Creating their own evenly spaced number line helps them understand and use this number line of integers to 32. Some students have a hard time visualizing past ten so the **EZTT** (EZ Times Table) gives them a visual scale of numbers where they can add several numbers on their big number line. (e.g. Have the students count down boxes as they add numbers: 3 + 4 + 5 + 6 + 7 = (25)

This number, One, can be thought of as the King of numbers. All other whole numbers are descendants of counting by Ones. One is a small increment, but it is crucially important.

EZ TIMES TABLE

Odd Numbers				1	Even Numbers			
				1				
				2				
				3				
				4				
				5				
				6				
				7				
				8				
				9				
				10				
				11				
				12				
				13				
				14				
				15				
				16				
				17				
				18				
				19				
				20				
				21				
				22				
				23				
				24				
				25				
				26				
				27				
				28				
				29				
				30				
				31				
				32				

Use the Ones column to multiply the Fives, Sevens, Nines, and Tens.

The Ones Table ©Thomas Biesanz 2007 www.eztimestable.com

THE TWOS

➤ Put a big 2 above the right gray column.

➤ Write the numbers 2, 4, 6, 8, and 0 going down the first five boxes in the right gray column, on the right side of the dotted line.

➤ Repeat the 2, 4, 6, 8, 0 pattern all the way down the right side of the dotted line, ending with a 4.

Your Table now looks like the one on the right.

To create the Table, turn to page 14 now.

Additional information:

The student is creating the numbers 2-64 in the right gray column. This page and the Table on the right are an intermediate step in creating the Twos column when you turn the page.

In this pattern method, the two numbers on both sides of the dotted line will create the Twos column. Kids love patterns and enjoy the adventure as the numbers unfold.

Accuracy is very important because the Twos contain the answers for most multiplication problems. Doing the Twos as a pattern is helpful for avoiding mistakes in counting by Twos, for teaching pattern recognition, and showing students how to rely on the many patterns in numbers to make it easier.

SEE NEXT PAGE: Counting by Twos is a good exercise and the student can go back and forth with the **Ones and Twos to double any number, or half any number** (12 + 12 = 24, 13 X 2 = 26, ½ of 28 = 14, 30 / 2 = 15). The student can pick any number in the Ones and multiply by 2 (double it) by looking in the Twos, or divide any number in the Twos column by 2 (half of the number) by looking in the Ones column. Have students do many fun problems doubling and halving.

EZ TIMES TABLE

				Odd Numbers	**1**	**2**	Even Numbers				
					1	2					
					2	4					
					3	6					
					4	8					
					5	0					
					6	2					
					7	4					
					8	6					
					9	8					
					10	0					
					11	2					
					12	4					
					13	6					
					14	8					
					15	0					
					16	2					
					17	4					
					18	6					
					19	8					
					20	0					
					21	2					
					22	4					
					23	6					
					24	8					
					25	0					
					26	2					
					27	4					
					28	6					
					29	8					
					30	0					
					31	2					
					32	4					

Use the Ones column to multiply the Fives, Sevens, Nines, and Tens.

The Twos-A Table copyright©Thomas Biesanz www.eztimestable.com

THE TWOS
(continued)

➢ Now you can create 10, 20, 30, 40, 50, and 60 by putting 1-6 in front of the six zeros.

➢ This is followed by writing 1 on the left side of the dotted line between 10 and 20, writing 2 between 20 and 30,... and then two 6's to create 62 and 64.

You have created the even numbers from 2 to 64.

To continue the Table, turn to page 16 now.

Additional information:

This column is a tree that the even numbers are built on. This means that when multiplying by 2, 4, 6, and 8, you will look in the Twos column for the answer. To multiply a number by two, find the number in the Ones column and look in the Twos column next to it for the answer. The student should do several multiplication-by-Two and dividing-by-two problems going back and forth between the Ones and Twos columns.

If one or both of the single digit numbers you are multiplying is even, **the answer will be found in the Twos column that contains all even numbers. This is ¾ of the multiplication table.**

Even times even equals an even number   E x E = E   (6 X 8 = 48)
Even times odd equals an even number   E x O = E   (4 X 9 = 36)
Odd times even equals an even number   O x E = E   (7 X 2 = 14)
Only an odd number times an odd number results in an odd number.

The number 64 should end up in the last box of the Twos column. If it is not there, look for a mistake in the patterns and correct it. The dotted line down the middle helps clarify these patterns. Patterns make multiplying more transparent. It is getting to know numbers like friends, where you notice little things that make them special.

The even numbers 2-64, next to the Ones, help the student see a scale of these larger numbers. It is like two maps, one scaled 1 inch = 1 mile and another scaled at 1/2 inch = 1 mile.

EZ TIMES TABLE

				Odd Numbers	**1**	**2**	Even Numbers			
					1	2				
					2	4				
					3	6				
					4	8				
					5	10				
					6	12				
					7	14				
					8	16				
					9	18				
					10	20				
					11	22				
					12	24				
					13	26				
					14	28				
					15	30				
					16	32				
					17	34				
					18	36				
					19	38				
					20	40				
					21	42				
					22	44				
					23	46				
					24	48				
					25	50				
					26	52				
					27	54				
					28	56				
					29	58				
					30	60				
					31	62				
					32	64				

Use the Ones column to multiply the Fives, Sevens, Nines, and Tens.

The Twos Table ©Thomas Biesanz 2007 www.eztimestable.com

THE THREES

- ➤ In the column to the left of the Ones, put a big 3 above this column.

- ➤ Put a 3 in the same row as the 3 in the Ones column. Directly above the 3 you just put in the Threes column, there are two empty boxes. Place a dot in these boxes.

- ➤ Look at the pattern you have just created (dot, dot, 3).

- ➤ Continue all the way down this column with this pattern of • • 3, • • 3, • • 3, • • 3, etc.

To continue the Table, turn to page 18 now.

Additional information:

The Threes are on the left of the Ones, because they are **odd numbers.** This Table helps reinforce the concept of odd and even numbers and shows the similarities and patterns that show up in each. It also shows how they relate.

The dots are just space holders and help define the pattern, and the Threes create groupings of threes in the Ones column. We are adding by Threes. This, of course, is multiplying but **with this Table we can go back and forth between adding and multiplying.** This anchors the process of multiplication. I have students confirm that two groupings of 3 (the second 3) is by the 6 in the ones column (2 X 3 = 6), the third 3 is by the 9 (3 X 3 = 9), etc. until the tenth 3 is found next to 30. Multiplication by Threes is just adding by Threes.

Do multiplication-by-three problems. To multiply 7 X 3, count down to the seventh 3 and find the number in the same row in the Ones column, 21, for the answer. Do enough problems that the student understands how to find the answers and that they are adding by Threes. Counting down is eliminated on the next page when the student labels each three with a number. Understanding this page makes the next page a simple clarification of what the student is already doing.

My mission in life is to create a world of deep play. Introducing patterns, fun, and movement enhances right-brain learning. The pattern of Threes become a **waltz**, and I sing while emphasizing the **Three** (1, 2, **3**,   1, 2, **3**, 1, 2, **3**) or (*dot, dot, **THREE**,   dot, dot, **THREE**,   dot, dot, **THREE...***)

EZ TIMES TABLE

			Odd Numbers	1	2	Even Numbers			
			3	1	2				
			•	1	2				
			•	2	4				
			3	3	6				
			•	4	8				
			•	5	10				
			3	6	12				
			•	7	14				
			•	8	16				
			3	9	18				
			•	10	20				
			•	11	22				
			3	12	24				
			•	13	26				
			•	14	28				
			3	15	30				
			•	16	32				
			•	17	34				
			3	18	36				
			•	19	38				
			•	20	40				
			3	21	42				
			•	22	44				
			•	23	46				
			3	24	48				
			•	25	50				
			•	26	52				
			3	27	54				
			•	28	56				
			•	29	58				
			3	30	60				
			•	31	62				
			•	32	64				

Use the Ones column to multiply the Fives, Sevens, Nines, and Tens.

The Threes-A Table copyright©Thomas Biesanz www.eztimestable.com

THE THREES
(continued)

> ➢ After the first 3 you wrote in the Threes column, put a small x1, after the second 3 put a small x2.

> ➢ Continue down until you have a 3x10 in the same row as 30 in the Ones column.

To continue the Table, turn to page 20 now.

To continue the Table, turn to page 20 now.

Additional information:

These small x1, x2, etc numbers are not necessary. Feel free to skip or delay this page depending on the student. The answer for each 3 is in the Ones column. The student counts down which number is in the Ones column by the third 3, by the fourth 3, etc.. Enjoy doing multiplication from the Threes pattern. After a while of counting down, introduce this page as a clarification of what they are aleady doing. If done too early, this page become a confusing element rather than a simplication. Once they make sense to the student, they establish this addition as multiplication. These x1, x2, x3's makes multiplying easier because the student no longer has to count down to the eighth 3. They look for the 3x8 and find the answer, 24. This page will also come in handy when we look at factors later in the book.

Now that we have established that **we can do either addition by threes or multiplication by threes in this column**, we can focus on multiplication. We can always go back to adding by threes, and it anchors our multiplication. It is now easy to go down to the fifth 3 and see that it is 15 or that the eighth 3 is 24. The student is creating a calculator that works and they can see how it works.

The student can also start to use their understanding to figure out answers. Students can start shifting up or down from the multiplication facts that they know. For example, if students know that the fifth 3 is 15, the sixth 3 can be determined by going down three boxes from 15 to find 18. They can know that the tenth 3 is 30, then count up three boxes to find that 3 times 9 is 27. Because it is based on the Ones (still visible) and counting by Threes, many students who had been intimidated by multiplication find it easy to learn with this table.

EZ TIMES TABLE

			Odd Numbers 3	1	2	Even Numbers			
			•	1	2				
			•	2	4				
			3 x1	3	6				
			•	4	8				
			•	5	10				
			3 x2	6	12				
			•	7	14				
			•	8	16				
			3 x3	9	18				
			•	10	20				
			•	11	22				
			3 x4	12	24				
			•	13	26				
			•	14	28				
			3 x5	15	30				
			•	16	32				
			•	17	34				
			3 x6	18	36				
			•	19	38				
			•	20	40				
			3 x7	21	42				
			•	22	44				
			•	23	46				
			3 x8	24	48				
			•	25	50				
			•	26	52				
			3 x9	27	54				
			•	28	56				
			•	29	58				
			3 x10	30	60				
			•	31	62				
			•	32	64				

Use the Ones column to multiply the Fives, Sevens, Nines, and Tens.

The Threes Table copyright©Thomas Biesanz www.eztimestable.com

THE FOURS

- ➤ Put a big **4** above the column to the right of the Twos.

- ➤ In the column to the right of the Twos, put a **4** in the same row as the **4** in the Twos column.

- ➤ Above the **4** you just put in the Fours column, there is one empty box. Put a dot in that box.

- ➤ Notice that you have a dot and then a 4. This is your pattern. Continue it all the way down the column:
  ● 4 ● 4 ● 4 ● 4 ... (... means continue this pattern)

- ➤ After the first 4, put a small **x1**, after the second 4 put a small **x2**. Continue down until you have a **4 x10** by the 40 in the Twos column.

To continue the Table, turn to page 22 now.

Additional information:

This is the Fours column. We find the answers by counting down the 4's and looking in the Twos column for the answer.

We establish it to the right of the Twos because it is the next even number. **The pattern relationship between Two and Four is set up**. Students notice that every other Two has a Four next to it. Two 2's are a four. This establishes a trust in the way the two columns relate. We are also counting by Fours.

We look for our answers to even numbers in the Twos column. I sometimes ask a student to see that the second 4 is in the same row as the 8 in the Twos column: $4 + 4 = 8$ and $4 \times 2 = 8$. The third 4 in the Fours column is by the 12 in the Twos column because $4 + 4 + 4 = 12$ and $4 \times 3 = 12$. Continue to multiply-by-four until they discover that the tenth four is by the 40 ($4 \times 10 = 40$). This helps them confirm that this system works and multiplication makes sense. Students can, and do, continue down to 4_{x16} in the same row as 64 in the Twos. This visual way to go back and forth between addition and multiplication is one of the strengths that help students understand this Table and multiplication.

Again we can skip the step of x1, x2, x3, x4, etc., until the student has done many multiplication problems by counting down 4's and finding the answer in the Twos column.

EZ TIMES TABLE

			Odd Numbers 3	1	2	Even Numbers 4			
			•	1	2	•			
			•	2	4	4 x1			
			3 x1	3	6	•			
			•	4	8	4 x2			
			•	5	10	•			
			3 x2	6	12	4 x3			
			•	7	14	•			
			•	8	16	4 x4			
			3 x3	9	18	•			
			•	10	20	4 x5			
			•	11	22	•			
			3 x4	12	24	4 x6			
			•	13	26	•			
			•	14	28	4 x7			
			3 x5	15	30	•			
			•	16	32	4 x8			
			•	17	34	•			
			3 x6	18	36	4 x9			
			•	19	38	•			
			•	20	40	4 x10			
			3 x7	21	42	•			
			•	22	44	4			
			•	23	46	•			
			3 x8	24	48	4			
			•	25	50	•			
			•	26	52	4			
			3 x9	27	54	•			
			•	28	56	4			
			•	29	58	•			
			3 x10	30	60	4			
			•	31	62	•			
			•	32	64	4			

Use the Ones column to multiply the Fives, Sevens, Nines, and Tens.

The Fours EZ Table copyright©Thomas Biesanz www.eztimestable.com

THE SIXES

➤ In the column to the right of the Fours, put a big 6 above this column.

➤ Put a 6 in the same row as the 6 in the Twos column.

➤ Above the 6 you just put in the Sixes column, there are two empty boxes. Put a dot in those boxes.

➤ Now in the Sixes column, you have two dots and a 6. This is your pattern. Continue it ALL the way DOWN the column: • • 6 • • 6 • • 6 • • 6 • • 6 etc.

➤ After the first 6, put a small x1, after the second 6 put a small x2. Continue down until you have a 6 x10 in the same row as the 60 in the Twos column.

To continue the Table, turn to page 24 now.

Additional information:

By this time many students are actively looking for the pattern, and start putting a 6 in every third box before I say anything. I let them choose to use dots or empty spaces, but my experience is that there is more accuracy with the dots.

The sixes are another Waltz pattern (• • 6, • • 6, • • 6,) Sometimes I point out, or students notice the visual pattern, that **Sixes are in the same rows with the Threes column** all the way down (same rows). This can open a curious discussion about how Threes and Sixes are alike. This will also show up in the **EZ RULER Table** in the back of the book.

I will sometimes ask, as I move my pencil point to the second six, "So, two sixes are _____?" They follow the pencil tip down to the second six and over to the Twos column for the answer of **12**. I may ask, "And three sixes are _____? Four sixes?" (I watch them count down the sixes). I ask them to check 10 sixes (the tenth 6) and they know it all works with an answer of **60**.

EZ TIMES TABLE

		Odd Numbers		1	2	Even Numbers	
			3			4	6
			•	1	2	•	•
			•	2	4	4 x1	•
			3 x1	3	6	•	6 x1
			•	4	8	4 x2	•
			•	5	10	•	•
			3 x2	6	12	4 x3	6 x2
			•	7	14	•	•
			•	8	16	4 x4	•
			3 x3	9	18	•	6 x3
			•	10	20	4 x5	•
			•	11	22	•	•
			3 x4	12	24	4 x6	6 x4
			•	13	26	•	•
			•	14	28	4 x7	•
			3 x5	15	30	•	6 x5
			•	16	32	4 x8	•
			•	17	34	•	•
			3 x6	18	36	4 x9	6 x6
			•	19	38	•	•
			•	20	40	4 x10	•
			3 x7	21	42	•	6 x7
			•	22	44	4	•
			•	23	46	•	•
			3 x8	24	48	4	6 x8
			•	25	50	•	•
			•	26	52	4	•
			3 x9	27	54	•	6 x9
			•	28	56	4	•
			•	29	58	•	•
			3 x10	30	60	4	6 x10
			•	31	62	•	•
			•	32	64	4	•

Use the Ones column to multiply the Fives, Sevens, Nines, and Tens.

The Sixes Table copyright©Thomas Biesanz www.eztimestable.com

THE EIGHTS

- ➢ In the column to the right of the Sixes, put a big 8 above this column.
- ➢ Put an 8 in the same row as the 8 in the Twos column.
- ➢ Above the 8 you just put in the Eights column, there are three empty boxes. Put a dot in those boxes.
- ➢ Now in this Eights column, you have three dots and then an 8. Look at this new pattern.
- ➢ Continue it DOWN to the bottom of the column:
- ➢ • • • 8 • • • 8 • • • 8 • • • 8 etc.
- ➢ After the first 8, put a small ₓ1, after the second 8 put a small ₓ2. Continue down until you have a 8 ₓ8 in the same row as the 64 in the Twos column.

To continue the Table, turn to page 26 now.

Additional information:

This first 8 is in the fourth box down. Those first three dots are in the same rows as the **2, 4**, and **6** in the Twos column.

Again, by the time they have put the first **8** in place, many kids will notice the enen number patterns and **ASK ME, "So, this pattern is dot, dot, dot, 8?"** "Yes." I emphasize the dot, dot, dot (3 dots) part of the pattern so they create the pattern accurately. I bring Beethoven into the pattern: (emphasis on the fourth sound)
Da, Da, Da, **Dum**, becomes Dot, dot, dot, **8**. Continue it down the column.

The students learn by seeing the patterns visually. Some students will catch another pattern, but if not, I let them get about halfway down the column and say something like, **"Notice that every other four is an eight!"** or "Two fours equal an eight?" I confirm with the student that 8 + 8 = 16 (The second 8 is at 16 in the Twos column: 8 X 2 = 16). The eighth 8 should be in the bottom row. (8 X 8 = 64). This relationship between the Fours and Eights will also show up in the **EZ Ruler Table** in the back of the book.

Repeating ones-digit pattern for the Eights is 8, 6, 4, 2 and 0. This is the opposite pattern on the Twos column (2, 4, 6, 8, 0).

EZ TIMES TABLE

			Odd Numbers 3	1	2	Even Numbers 4	6	8	
			•	1	2	•	•	•	
			•	2	4	4 x1	•	•	
			3 x1	3	6	•	6 x1	•	
			•	4	8	4 x2	•	8 x1	
			•	5	10	•	•	•	
			3 x2	6	12	4 x3	6 x2	•	
			•	7	14	•	•	•	
			•	8	16	4 x4	•	8 x2	
			3 x3	9	18	•	6 x3	•	
			•	10	20	4 x5	•	•	
			•	11	22	•	•	•	
			3 x4	12	24	4 x6	6 x4	8 x3	
			•	13	26	•	•	•	
			•	14	28	4 x7	•	•	
			3 x5	15	30	•	6 x5	•	
			•	16	32	4 x8	•	8 x4	
			•	17	34	•	•	•	
			3 x6	18	36	4 x9	6 x6	•	
			•	19	38	•	•	•	
			•	20	40	4 x10	•	8 x5	
			3 x7	21	42	•	6 x7	•	
			•	22	44	4	•	•	
			•	23	46	•	•	•	
			3 x8	24	48	4	6 x8	8 x6	
			•	25	50	•	•	•	
			•	26	52	4	•	•	
			3 x9	27	54	•	6 x9	•	
			•	28	56	4	•	8 x7	
			•	29	58	•	•	•	
			3 x10	30	60	4	6 x10	•	
			•	31	62	•	•	•	
			•	32	64	4	•	8 x8	

Use the Ones column to multiply the Fives, Sevens, Nines, and Tens.

The EightsTable copyright©Thomas Biesanz www.eztimestable.com

THE TENS

In the column to the right of the Eights, we will use a shortcut, since the Tens are Easy.

➢ Put a big 10 above the far right column.

➢ On the left side of the dotted line, put the numbers 1-10 in the ten boxes.

➢ On the right side of the dotted line put a zero in each box creating the numbers 10-100.

To continue the Table, turn to page 28 now.

Additional information:

We could put the numbers 10-100 in the ten boxes, but the method above adds to the pattern focus, which is helpful for all students.

We could also do ● ● ● ● 10 (dot, dot, dot, dot, ten). The pattern would work, although four dots can create errors. But we can use the shortcut because any student who can't count by tens can write the numbers 1-10 and add a zero to each number. Practically, the **short columns (ten rows)** work and we will use them for the Fives in the same way.

All the short columns are connected to the Ones column. The first through tenth boxes are connected to the numbers 1-10 in the same row of the Ones. The student can either count down the number of boxes (The fifth Ten is 50) or go down to the 5 in the Ones and then find 50 in the same row of the Tens. We will also use short columns for the Fives, Sevens and Nines, but create these in different ways.

After we complete the basic EZ Times Table, you can explore using the ● ● ● ● 10 pattern for the Tens on the *Times Line Table* in **Part 2** of the book. We will also use dot patterns to expand the other short columns on page 64, but that is optional in the advanced section and of no concern here.

EZ TIMES TABLE

Odd Numbers			Even Numbers			
3	**1**	**2**	**4**	**6**	**8**	**10**
•	1	2	•	•	•	1 0
•	2	4	4 x1	•	•	2 0
3 x1	3	6	•	6 x1	•	3 0
•	4	8	4 x2	•	8 x1	4 0
•	5	1 0	•	•	•	5 0
3 x2	6	1 2	4 x3	6 x2	•	6 0
•	7	1 4	•	•	•	7 0
•	8	1 6	4 x4	•	8 x2	8 0
3 x3	9	1 8	•	6 x3	•	9 0
•	1 0	2 0	4 x5	•	•	10 0
•	1 1	2 2	•	•	•	
3 x4	1 2	2 4	4 x6	6 x4	8 x3	
•	1 3	2 6	•	•	•	
•	1 4	2 8	4 x7	•	•	
3 x5	1 5	3 0	•	6 x5	•	
•	1 6	3 2	4 x8	•	8 x4	
•	1 7	3 4	•	•	•	
3 x6	1 8	3 6	4 x9	6 x6	•	
•	1 9	3 8	•	•	•	
•	2 0	4 0	4 x10	•	8 x5	
3 x7	2 1	4 2	•	6 x7	•	
•	2 2	4 4	4	•	•	
•	2 3	4 6	•	•	•	
3 x8	2 4	4 8	4	6 x8	8 x6	
•	2 5	5 0	•	•	•	
•	2 6	5 2	4	•	•	
3 x9	2 7	5 4	•	6 x9	•	
•	2 8	5 6	4	•	8 x7	
•	2 9	5 8	•	•	•	
3 x10	3 0	6 0	4	6 x10	•	
•	3 1	6 2	•	•	•	
•	3 2	6 4	4	•	8 x8	

Use the Ones column to multiply the Fives, Sevens, Nines, and Tens.

The Tens Table copyright©Thomas Biesanz www.eztimestable.com

THE FIVES

- ➤ Put a big 5 above the column to the left of the Threes.
- ➤ In the column, count down by 5's to 50 (5, 10, 15, 20, 25, 30, 35, 40, 45, 50).

To continue the Table, turn to page 30 now.

Additional information:

The Fives column is only ten rows and can be linked to the Ones column: "1 Five is 5" (pointing to the 1 in the Ones column and then the first empty box in the Fives), "2 Fives are 10 (pointing to the 2 in the Ones column and then the second empty box in the Fives), etc. The student writes 5 in the first box of the Fives column, then 10 in the second box, etc. They usually quickly respond, "Oh, I am counting by Fives!"

I have had a few young students who couldn't count by fives, but they could count up **to** 5. They used the Ones column to circle every fifth number to get up to 30 and could figure it out from there. This is another advantage of having the long number line to 32. They learned the Fives in the process.

The Fives, Sevens, and Nines are short, condensed columns like the Tens. The numbers 1-50 could be written out and then have the students find the pattern. At this point, however, the shorter version is trusted by the student.

A "problem" here is that some students become the energizer bunny (they like to keep going and going). Stop at 50, which gives 5 X 10 = 50, **OR** let them go down along the picture of the swimming 5 and his friends to a hundred or more, and let them have fun learning.

EZ TIMES TABLE

	Odd Numbers				Even Numbers			
	5	**3**	**1**	**2**	**4**	**6**	**8**	**10**
	5	•	1	2	•	•	•	1 0
	10	•	2	4	4 x1	•	•	2 0
	15	3 x1	3	6	•	6 x1	•	3 0
	20	•	4	8	4 x2	•	8 x1	4 0
	25	•	5	1 0	•	•	•	5 0
	30	3 x2	6	1 2	4 x3	6 x2	•	6 0
	35	•	7	1 4	•	•	•	7 0
	40	•	8	1 6	4 x4	•	8 x2	8 0
	45	3 x3	9	1 8	•	6 x3	•	9 0
	50	•	1 0	2 0	4 x5	•	•	10 0
		•	1 1	2 2	•	•	•	
		3 x4	1 2	2 4	4 x6	6 x4	8 x3	
		•	1 3	2 6	•	•	•	
		•	1 4	2 8	4 x7	•	•	
		3 x5	1 5	3 0	•	6 x5	•	
		•	1 6	3 2	4 x8	•	8 x4	
		•	1 7	3 4	•	•	•	
		3 x6	1 8	3 6	4 x9	6 x6	•	
		•	1 9	3 8	•	•	•	
		•	2 0	4 0	4 x10	•	8 x5	
		3 x7	2 1	4 2	•	6 x7	•	
		•	2 2	4 4	4	•	•	
		•	2 3	4 6	•	•	•	
		3 x8	2 4	4 8	4	6 x8	8 x6	
		•	2 5	5 0	•	•	•	
		•	2 6	5 2	4	•	•	
		3 x9	2 7	5 4	•	6 x9	•	
		•	2 8	5 6	4	•	8 x7	
		•	2 9	5 8	•	•	•	
		3 x10	3 0	6 0	4	6 x10	•	
		•	3 1	6 2	•	•	•	
		•	3 2	6 4	4	•	8 x8	

Use the Ones column to multiply the Fives, Sevens, Nines, and Tens.

The Fives Table ©Thomas Biesanz 2007 www.eztimestable.com

THE NINES
A step in creating the Nines

This Table is the first stage in creating the Nines.

➢ Put a big 9 above the far left column.

➢ Going down the left column, on the left side of the dotted line, place the numbers 0-9 in the ten boxes.

Your Table now looks like the one on the right.

To continue the Table, turn to page 32 now.

Additional information:

We are skipping the Sevens for now and moving to the Nines. There are **many interesting ways to approach Nines**, which could be big and intimidating numbers. We are again using 10 rows divided by a dotted line.

This method fits the Table and also establishes several patterns for learning the Nines. The first digit (the tens value) is always one number less than the number (in the Ones column) that you are multiplying by nine. I usually start by telling them this fact and the students help figure out that the one becomes a zero, the two becomes a one, the three turns into a two, etc., and suddenly they see the pattern and create the 0-9 pattern.

This is an intermediate step which will be finished on the next page. **This page is creating the tens-digit number of the Nines.** The two numbers on both sides of the dotted line will create multiplication by nine.

Looking at this simple pattern **allows students to quickly re-create the Nines** for problems or memorization. Smiles and nods show how much appreciation students have for this simple method. Turn the page to finish the pattern.

EZ TIMES TABLE

9		Odd Numbers 5	3	1	2	Even Numbers 4	6	8	10
0		5	•	1	2	•	•	•	1 0
1		10	•	2	4	4 x1	•	•	2 0
2		15	3 x1	3	6	•	6 x1	•	3 0
3		20	•	4	8	4 x2	•	8 x1	4 0
4		25	•	5	1 0	•	•	•	5 0
5		30	3 x2	6	1 2	4 x3	6 x2	•	6 0
6	☐	35	•	7	1 4	•	•	•	7 0
7		40	•	8	1 6	4 x4	•	8 x2	8 0
8		45	3 x3	9	1 8	•	6 x3	•	9 0
9		50	•	1 0	2 0	4 x5	•	•	10 0
			•	1 1	2 2	•	•	•	
			3 x4	1 2	2 4	4 x6	6 x4	8 x3	
			•	1 3	2 6	•	•	•	
			•	1 4	2 8	4 x7	•	•	
			3 x5	1 5	3 0	•	6 x5	•	
			•	1 6	3 2	4 x8	•	8 x4	
			•	1 7	3 4	•	•	•	
			3 x6	1 8	3 6	4 x9	6 x6	•	
			•	1 9	3 8	•	•	•	
			•	2 0	4 0	4 x10	•	8 x5	
			3 x7	2 1	4 2	•	6 x7	•	
			•	2 2	4 4	4	•	•	
			•	2 3	4 6	•	•	•	
			3 x8	2 4	4 8	4	6 x8	8 x6	
			•	2 5	5 0	•	•	•	
			•	2 6	5 2	4	•	•	
			3 x9	2 7	5 4	•	6 x9	•	
			•	2 8	5 6	4	•	8 x7	
			•	2 9	5 8	•	•	•	
			3 x10	3 0	6 0	4	6 x10	•	
			•	3 1	6 2	•	•	•	
			•	3 2	6 4	4	•	8 x8	

Use the Ones column to multiply the Fives, Sevens, Nines, and Tens.

The Nines-A Table copyright©Thomas Biesanz www.eztimestable.com

THE NINES
(continued)

➢ In the same bottom row as the 9 (tenth row in Nines column), write a 0 on the right side of the dotted line. Write 0-9 going **UP** on the right side of the dotted line.

To continue the Table, turn to page 34 now.

Additional information:

The two sides of the dotted line in the last column together make up the two digit Nines products.

Students like the patterns in nines. (0-9 down and 0-9 up along the dotted line). I also sometimes tell them that the two digits of the Nines add up to nine: (09, 18, 27, 36, 45, 54, 63, 72, 81, 90). This fact can be additional information, or they can create the second digit by figuring out what number is needed to add up to nine:

0+9=9
1+8=9
2+7=9
3+6=9
4+5=9
5+4=9
6+3=9
7+2=9
8+1=9
9+0=9

Add this understanding to the fact that the tens-digit is always one less than the number you are multipying by nine. "Cool" say many students.

Students quickly grasp from this Table that to multiply 9 X 7, **take one number less (6) for the tens digit, and follow that with the number that adds up to nine** (9-6=3) as the Ones digit. Answer: 63. Thus 9 X 5 would break down to two steps: 5-1=4 and 9-4=5. Answer: 45.

EZ TIMES TABLE

Odd Numbers				1	2	Even Numbers			
9	7	5	3			4	6	8	10
0 9	7	5	•	1	2	•	•	•	1 0
1 8	14	10	•	2	4	4 x1	•	•	2 0
2 7	21	15	3 x1	3	6	•	6 x1	•	3 0
3 6	28	20	•	4	8	4 x2	•	8 x1	4 0
4 5	35	25	•	5	10	•	•	•	5 0
5 4	42	30	3 x2	6	12	4 x3	6 x2	•	6 0
6 3	49	35	•	7	14	•	•	•	7 0
7 2	56	40	•	8	16	4 x4	•	8 x2	8 0
8 1	63	45	3 x3	9	18	•	6 x3	•	9 0
9 0	70	50	•	1 0	2 0	4 x5	•	•	10 0
			•	1 1	2 2	•	•	•	
			3 x4	1 2	2 4	4 x6	6 x4	8 x3	
			•	1 3	2 6	•	•	•	
			•	1 4	2 8	4 x7	•	•	
			3 x5	1 5	3 0	•	6 x5	•	
			•	1 6	3 2	4 x8	•	8 x4	
			•	1 7	3 4	•	•	•	
			3 x6	1 8	3 6	4 x9	6 x6	•	
			•	1 9	3 8	•	•	•	
			•	2 0	4 0	4 x10	•	8 x5	
			3 x7	2 1	4 2	•	6 x7	•	
			•	2 2	4 4	4	•	•	
			•	2 3	4 6	•	•	•	
			3 x8	2 4	4 8	4	6 x8	8 x6	
			•	2 5	5 0	•	•	•	
			•	2 6	5 2	4	•	•	
			3 x9	2 7	5 4	•	6 x9	•	
			•	2 8	5 6	4	•	8 x7	
			•	2 9	5 8	•	•	•	
			3 x10	3 0	6 0	4	6 x10	•	
			•	3 1	6 2	•	•	•	
			•	3 2	6 4	4	•	8 x8	

Use the Ones column to multiply the Fives, Sevens, Nines, and Tens.

The Nines Table ©Thomas Biesanz 2007 www.eztimestable.com

THE SEVENS

➤ The column to the left of the Fives is the Sevens. In the seventh box down, write the number 49.

To continue the Table, turn to page 36 now.

Additional information:

The reason that we only **have** to put one number in the Sevens column is that **7 X 7 is the only 7 multiplication fact that we can't find in the other columns. This is a good time to reinforce that all the numbers are reversible.** While building the Table, ask students to check their own answers by checking the reverse: the fourth 5 is 20 and the fifth 4 is 20. The eighth 3 is 24 and the third 8 is 24. After a series of checking these same answers out, they now understand the *commutative law* (4 x 3 = 3 x 4). The *commutative law* **states that reversing the numbers in multiplication and addition results in the same answer.**

7 X 1 is found in the Ones column as seven Ones are 7, and 7 X 2 is found in the Twos column since seven Twos are 14. All the other Sevens can be found in the other columns except seven Sevens. I strongly encourage students to fill in these missing numbers as an exercise in using the Table as well as becoming familiar with multiplication facts. The family of Sevens have been filled in on the right page.

The number 49 is the one number that students can memorize. I connect it with California being the Gold Rush State. Californians are the Forty-Niners. The students also know the football team, the 49ers. I tell students that finding the multiplication tables in their patterns is like finding **GOLD**.

Even this number (49) can be confirmed with the Table. 7 Sixes can be found by going down the Sixes column to 6x7 to point to 42 in the same row in the Twos column. Fill that number in the sixth box in the Sevens column (6 X 7 =   7 X 6). Then add 7 to 42 and put the sum (49) in the seventh box, which is in the same row as the 7 in the Ones column. You don't even need to remember 49 to complete the table!

Note: For a pattern way to create the Sevens, Look at page 55 in Advanced Patterns.

EZ TIMES TABLE

9	7	5	3	1	2	4	6	8	10
Odd Numbers					Even Numbers				
0 9	7	5	•	1	2	•	•	•	1 0
1 8	14	10	•	2	4	4 x1	•	•	2 0
2 7	21	15	3 x1	3	6	•	6 x1	•	3 0
3 6	28	20	•	4	8	4 x2	•	8 x1	4 0
4 5	35	25	•	5	10	•	•	•	5 0
5 4	42	30	3 x2	6	12	4 x3	6 x2	•	6 0
6 3	**49**	35	•	7	14	•	•	•	7 0
7 2	56	40	•	8	16	4 x4	•	8 x2	8 0
8 1	63	45	3 x3	9	18	•	6 x3	•	9 0
9 0	70	50	•	1 0	20	4 x5	•	•	10 0
			•	1 1	2 2	•	•	•	
			3 x4	1 2	2 4	4 x6	6 x4	8 x3	
			•	1 3	2 6	•	•	•	
			•	1 4	2 8	4 x7	•	•	
			3 x5	1 5	3 0	•	6 x5	•	
			•	1 6	3 2	4 x8	•	8 x4	
			•	1 7	3 4	•	•	•	
			3 x6	1 8	3 6	4 x9	6 x6	•	
			•	1 9	3 8	•	•	•	
			•	2 0	4 0	4 x10	•	8 x5	
			3 x7	2 1	4 2	•	6 x7	•	
			•	2 2	4 4	4	•	•	
			•	2 3	4 6	•	•	•	
			3 x8	2 4	4 8	4	6 x8	8 x6	
			•	2 5	5 0	•	•	•	
			•	2 6	5 2	4	•	•	
			3 x9	2 7	5 4	•	6 x9	•	
			•	2 8	5 6	4	•	8 x7	
			•	2 9	5 8	•	•	•	
			3 x10	3 0	6 0	4	6 x10	•	
			•	3 1	6 2	•	•	•	
			•	3 2	6 4	4	•	8 x8	

Use the Ones column to multiply the
Fives, Sevens, Nines, and Tens.

The Sevens-49 Table copyright©Thomas Biesanz www.eztimestable.com

THE ZEROS

➢ In the box in the bottom left corner of the EZ TIMES TABLE, write "0 X any number = 0" or "Zero times any number equals zero."

YIPPEE! You are done with the Table.

You can use it for multiplication problems, as well as addition, subtraction, division, and learning the times tables.

Go on to PART 2 and PART 3 for more ways to use the table, variations of the table and playing with patterns.

Additional information:

The number Zero is different from the other numbers. Count by Zeros! (0,0,0,0,0,0,0,0,0,0,0 etc.) Zero times any number needs special attention. The answer is always one of those zeros. It is a simple reality that **EVERY NUMBER TIMES ZERO EQUALS ZERO**. An alternate location on the table to put the Zeros would be to create an eleventh column, maybe to the right of the Tens, putting a big 0 above the column and 0 in each of the 32 boxes. Using the Ones column to multiply would still result with 0 for each product.

The whole multiplication table is now embedded in the Table. Students are amazed that it is so simple. Missing from the Table is 8 X 9, but it shows up in the Nines column as 9 X 8.

EZ TIMES TABLE

	Odd Numbers						Even Numbers			
9	7	5	3	1	2	4	6	8	10
0 9	7	5	•	1	2	•	•	•	1 0
1 8	14	10	•	2	4	4 x1	•	•	2 0
2 7	21	15	3 x1	3	6	•	6 x1	•	3 0
3 6	28	20	•	4	8	4 x2	•	8 x1	4 0
4 5	35	25	•	5	1 0	•	•	•	5 0
5 4	42	30	3 x2	6	1 2	4 x3	6 x2	•	6 0
6 3	49	35	•	7	1 4	•	•	•	7 0
7 2	56	40	•	8	1 6	4 x4	•	8 x2	8 0
8 1	63	45	3 x3	9	1 8	•	6 x3	•	9 0
9 0	70	50	•	1 0	2 0	4 x5	•	•	10 0

Use the Ones column to multiply the
Fives, Sevens, Nines, and Tens.

9	7	5	3	1	2	4	6	8	10
			•	1 1	2 2	•	•	•	
			3 x4	1 2	2 4	4 x6	6 x4	8 x3	
			•	1 3	2 6	•	•	•	
			•	1 4	2 8	4 x7	•	•	
			3 x5	1 5	3 0	•	6 x5	•	
			•	1 6	3 2	4 x8	•	8 x4	
			•	1 7	3 4	•	•	•	
			3 x6	1 8	3 6	4 x9	6 x6	•	
			•	1 9	3 8	•	•	•	
			•	2 0	4 0	4 x10	•	8 x5	
			3 x7	2 1	4 2	•	6 x7	•	
			•	2 2	4 4	4	•	•	
			•	2 3	4 6	•	•	•	
			3 x8	2 4	4 8	4	6 x8	8 x6	
			•	2 5	5 0	•	•	•	
			•	2 6	5 2	4	•	•	
			3 x9	2 7	5 4	•	6 x9	•	
			•	2 8	5 6	4	•	8 x7	
			•	2 9	5 8	•	•	•	
			3 x10	3 0	6 0	4	6 x10	•	
			•	3 1	6 2	•	•	•	
			•	3 2	6 4	4	•	8 x8	

Zero X any number = zero

Complete EZ Table ©Thomas Biesanz 2007 www.eztimestable.com

EASY TIMES

by Janet Jacobsen

If numbers make you feel numb and dumb,
here is a way to make them fun.
Just take a look at the open chart
and see the big "T", that's your start.

Now number down both sides of the "T".
On the left side write down 1, 2 , 3,
4, 5, 6, 7, 8, 9, oh,
repeating again on down the row.

On the right side 2, 4, 6, 8, oh,
And repeat again on down you go.
Add one's and two's making teens and twenties.
It's as easy as counting copper pennies.

Odd numbers go across the left top "T" line.
Write 1, 3, 5, 7, and then 9.
Even numbers go across the right side again,
2, 4, 6, 8 and then 10.

Now you have a big numbered "T".
Once you add dots you'll have the key
to finding patterns that are fun and easy to see
and will help you learn the times table effortlessly.

EZ TIMES TABLE

		Odd Numbers					Even Numbers			

Use the Ones column to multiply the Fives, Sevens, Nines, and Tens.

All Instructions on one page

1. **Put a big 1** above the left gray column. Going down the right side of the column, write the numbers 1, 2, 3, 4, 5, 6, 7 8, 9, 0, and repeat until you reach the bottom of the column.

2. Put a 1 in front of the first 0, a two in front of the second 0... Put 1's between the 1 and 2 on the left side, 2's between the 2 and 3, and 3 in front of the last 1 and 2. You have created the numbers 1-32. write the numbers 2, 4, 6, 8, 0, and repeat until you reach the bottom of the column.

3. Put a 1 in front of the first 0, a two in front of the second 0... Put 1's between the 1 and 2 on the left side, 2's between the 2 and 3..., and 6 in front of the last 2 and 4. You have created the numbers 2-64.

4. **Put a big 3** above the column to the left of the Ones. Put a 3 in the same row as the 3 in the Ones column. Above the 3 you just put in the Threes column, there are two empty boxes. Place a dot in these boxes. Look at the pattern you have just created. (dot, dot, 3). Continue all the way down this column with this pattern of ● ● 3, ● ● 3, ● ● 3...

5. **Put a big 4** in the column to the right of the Twos. Put a 4 in the same row as the 4 in the Twos column. Above the 4 you just put in the Fours column, there is one empty box. Put a dot in that box. Notice that you have a pattern of a dot and then a 4. Continue this pattern all the way down the column: ● 4, ● 4, ● 4, ● 4, ● 4, ● 4...

6. **Put a big 6** above the column to the right of the Fours. In this column, put a 6 in the same row as the 6 in the Twos column. Above the 6 you just put in the Sixes column, there are two empty boxes. Put a dot in those boxes. Now in the Sixes column, you have two dots and a 6. This is your pattern. Continue it all the way down the column: ● ● 6, ● ● 6, ● ● 6,   ● ● 6, ● ● 6...

7. **Put a big 8** above the column to the right of the Sixes. Put an 8 in the same row as the 8 in the Twos column. Above the 8 you just put in the Eights column, there are three empty boxes. Put a dot in those boxes. Now in this Eights column, you have three dots and then an 8. Look at this new pattern. Continue it **down** to the bottom of the column:● ● ● 8, ● ● ● 8, ● ● ● 8, ● ● ● 8...

8. **Put a big 10** in the column to the right of the Eights. Here we will use a shortcut. On the left side, put the numbers 1-10. On the right side, put a 0 in each of the ten boxes. You have created the numbers 10-100.

9. **Put a big 5** above the column to the left of the Threes. In the column to the left of the Threes, count down by 5's to 50 (5, 10, 15, 20, 25, 30, 35, 40, 45, 50).

10. **Put a big 9** above the far left column. The Nines column has 10 rows divided by a dotted line. Write down the left side of the dotted line the numbers 0-9. In the same row as the 9 at the bottom, write a 0 on the right side of the dotted line. Write 0-9 going UP.

11. **Put a big 7** above the column to the left of the Fives. In the seventh box down, write the number 49.

12. **In the box** in the bottom left corner of the **EZ TIMES TABLE** write "*0 X any number = 0*" or "*Zero times any number equals zero*."

13. **To eliminate counting** the numbers using dot patterns, place a little x1 in the corner of the first 3, a little x2 in the corner of the second 3, a little x3 in the corner of the third 3.... Repeat for the Fours, Sixes and Eights.

CONGRATULATIONS!!!!!!!!!
You have created the EZ Times Table

I believe everybody should create an EZ Times Table.
This next section describes ways to use the EZ Times Table.

LEARNING WITH THE EZ TIMES TABLE

ADDITION & SUBTRACTION

The students have made their own number line to 32 by creating the Ones column. Even spaced boxes appeal to the right side of the brain and they can accurately add by moving down the number line. A young student feels comfortable using the number line because they have created it themselves. Creating the Ones also gives them experience writing the numbers in order. The fact that it goes up to 32 allows them to add a series of numbers by continuing down the boxes (3 + 4 + 6 + 8 + 21).

Carrying tens, which sometimes creates confusion, can be delayed until after they **understand the concept of addition.** After adding by moving down boxes on the long number line to 32 for a while, the principle of carrying makes sense and can be easily added.

Some experts feel that it is **beneficial to move from addition directly into multiplication**, which is just a form of adding similar numbers. To move from addition to subtraction to multiplication can present each as a whole new subject and can create confusion. **These Tables teach addition and multiplication with the same format.**

Whenever **subtraction** is introduced, it is understood as moving up the Ones column instead of down. It is clear that it is the reverse of addition.

DIVISION

Once the students are clear about using the EZ Times Table for multiplication, they can understand division using the Table. **Division can be seen, understood, and practiced as REVERSE multiplication.**

The first task is to **find where the "answer" would be** if it was a multiplication problem. Dividing by 2 is accomplished by finding the number in the Twos column and looking in the same row in the Ones. To divide a number by Five, Seven, Nine, or Ten, find the number in the appropriate column and look in the Ones column for the answer.

Answers when dividing by Four, Six, and Eight are in the Twos column. Let's look at 54 divided by 6. Since six is an even number, we look in the Twos column for "answer" 54. In the same row as the 54 in the Twos column is a 6 in the Sixes column. Count which 6 this is, or look at the little x9 behind it. It is the ninth 6. Therefore 54 ÷ 6 is 9. The EZ times Table clarifies the process and the relation between multiplication and division.

We can even do remainders. Let's look at 26 divided by 4. Since the four is an even number, we look in the Twos column for 26. In the same row, the Fours column has a dot. The closest 4 (that is smaller) is the sixth 4 next to 24. 26 ÷ 4 = 6 with a remainder of 2, or 6 ½. **Students can understand what half means** since they can see that 26 is halfway between the sixth and seventh 6. This engages the right side of the brain to understand fractions as a spacial reality (half of a box).

If a number (the dividend) is **divided by a number in a short column, the answer is in the Ones column** in the same row as the dividend. Let's divide 63 by 9. we would look in the Nines column for the "answer" since we are dividing by 9. We find 63 or the nearest lower number. It is in the seventh box in the nines column, so the answer is 63 ÷ 9 = 7. It is also in the same row as the 7 in the Ones column. Students now understand that multiplication and division are opposites and that they can work either way with the Chart.

SQUARES

Finding the first One, the second Two, the third Three, the fourth Four, the fifth Five... adds a dimension to squares that creates interest and promotes understanding of what a square number is. Ones, Twos, Threes, etc. are capitalized because they are families where the individual numbers in each set are at home. The Fives include 5, 10, 15, 20, and **25, which is the fifth and square number of the Five family.**

FRACTIONS

Fractions are another way of seeing division with some multiplication thrown in. Start with ¼ of 12. Since 12 is an even number, find 12 in the Twos column. One fourth means that you are dividing by 4. Looking in the Fours column next to the 12 in the Ones column, you see that the third 4 is there. You can also divide the Ones column down to twelve in four equal parts (three numbers each). **This adds another visual, right-brain dimension.** ¼ x 12 = 3. I like using ¼ because it is also called a quarter. For 2/4 (two quarters) of 12, I hold up a real quarter and ask, "If one quarter (¼) is worth 3, then two quarters are worth _____?" I hold up two quarters and the students see that two quarters (each worth 3) are worth 6. "And three quarters are worth _____?" They see that three quarters (each worth 3) are worth 9. Once the principle is established, fractions are easy work.

FACTORS

Factors can easily be found for any number by finding the number on the EZTT. Looking to see what column they are in tells the student one factor of the number. Another can be found by looking in the Ones and Twos column in the same row. 24, next to 6_{x4} shows that 6 and 4 are factors of that number.

PLACE VALUE

Students have used Ones-digits and Tens-digits in patterns when they created the Ones, Twos, Nines and Tens. See **Ones-units on page 54**. Kids are just learning names for what they already are using.

PRIME NUMBERS

The *Times Line Table* (page 65) is a great overview to explore **prime numbers**. These are numbers that can only be divided by 1 and themselves. Accepting that 2, 3, 5, and 7 fit this definition, they are circled (they show up as factors of themselves). Go down the Ones column and see that 11 has only dots (no factor numbers) in that row. 13, 17, 19, 23, 29, 31, 37, 41, 43, & 47 also have only dots in their row. These numbers are also circled. Because they have no factors, they are prime numbers. The Table could be continued to 100 or more as a project to learn about factors and prime numbers using this right-brain overview. Could we find all prime numbers by continuing this chart?

USING THE EZ TIMES TABLE WITH OTHER LEARNING METHODS

The EZ TIMES TABLE appeals to several learning strategies. It can stand alone as a method of teaching math, but it also is reinforced by combining it with other methods.

Using it with flash cards can become a game to find the answers in two different ways for each card. This increases confidence and locks in the actual multiplication facts as students learn their way around the Table.

The **EZTT works well with manipulatives** too. As you move each pair of blocks (or other manipulatives), go down one box in the Twos column with a finger or pencil. The Twos column will keep count of the total number of blocks and Ones column will keep track of the number of pairs.

Now double up the pairs and move the groups of four blocks down as groups. In the Fours column, point to the first 4 with this group, and then the second 4 with the second group of 4 blocks. Moving over to the Twos column shows that you have 8 blocks and the Ones column shows that this is your second group of 4 blocks. Moving the tenth group of four is done as you point to the tenth 4. This shows the student that he has moved 40 blocks (in the Twos column) and that this is his tenth group of four blocks (by counting the 4's or looking at the small x10 after that 4).

The same method works for the Threes, Sixes, and Eights. For the Fives, Sevens, Nines, and Tens, go down one box with each corresponding set of blocks moved.

The EZ Times Table also works well with counting rectangles on graph paper. On graph paper you can give added meanings to each of the families of Ones, Twos, Threes, Fours, etc. with rectangles one wide, two wide, three wide, etc. and then going to the **EZTT** to get totals for each row of squares.

WORKSHEET

The next two pages are a two sided worksheet that can be used to focus on using the Table while, or after creating the Table. It can also be used in a class for fast students who are waiting for their peers to finish a column.

NAME _____ DATE _____

ONES	TWOS	THREES	FOURS	SIXES
8 x 1 =	6 x 2 =	3 x 5 =	8 x 4 =	9 x 6 =
6 x 1 =	3 x 2 =	3 x 8 =	4 x 4 =	8 x 6 =
3 x 1 =	9 x 2 =	3 x 2 =	4 x 4 =	6 x 4 =
9 x 1 =	8 x 2 =	2 x 3 =	4 x 7 =	6 x 6 =
1 x 4 =	2 x 4 =	3 x 7 =	4 x 1 =	6 x 7 =
1 x 2 =	2 x 2 =	3 x 9 =	4 x 2 =	6 x 1 =
1 x 7 =	2 x 7 =	3 x 1 =	6 x 4 =	6 x 8 =
1 x 1 =	2 x 1 =	1 x 3 =	3 x 4 =	6 x 3 =
6 + 2 =	2 x 18 =	4 x 3 =	9 x 4 =	3 x 6 =
7 + 4 =	2 x 23 =	3 x 6 =	7 x 4 =	6 x 2 =
14 + 3 =	14 / 2 =	8 x 3 =	5 x 4 =	7 x 6 =
15 + 6 =	18 / 2 =	9 x 3 =	2 x 4 =	5 x 6 =
12 + 3 + 4 =	26 / 2 =			
22 + 5 + 2 =	30 / 2 =			

EIGHTS	TENS	FIVES	NINES	SEVENS
8 x 5 =	10 x 5 =	8 x 5 =	9 x 9 =	9 x 7 =
8 x 8 =	10 x 8 =	5 x 5 =	8 x 9 =	8 x 7 =
8 x 2 =	10 x 2 =	5 x 8 =	9 x 4 =	7 x 4 =
2 x 8 =	2 x 10 =	5 x 7 =	9 x 9 =	7 x 7 =
8 x 7 =	10 x 7 =	5 x 1 =	9 x 7 =	7 x 7 =
8 x 9 =	10 x 9 =	5 x 2 =	9 x 1 =	7 x 1 =
8 x 1 =	10 x 1 =	6 X 5 =	9 x 8 =	7 x 2 =
1 x 8 =	1 x 10 =	3 x 5 =	9 x 3 =	7 x 3 =
4 x 8 =	4 x 10 =	9 x 5 =	3 x 9 =	3 x 7 =
5 x 8 =	10 x 3 =	5 x 6 =	5 x 9 =	6 x 7 =
8 x 3 =	10 x 6 =	5 x 3 =	7 x 9 =	7 x 5 =
6 x 8 =	10 x 4 =	7 X 5 =	4 x 9 =	7 x 8 =
8 x 4 =	8 x 10 =	4 x 5 =	6 x 9 =	7 x 6 =
3 x 8 =	6 x 10 =	9 x 5 =	2 x 9 =	5 x 7 =

PLAYING WITH THE EZ TIMES TABLE

Any multiplication workbook or page of **problems can be used with the Chart**. The following page starts with one digit multiplication. Copy this for your class or use your own. The students have created the times table and they are amazed that all the answers to one-digit multiplication are in this simple Table. It is very important to use the **EZTT** with many problems until they understand that all multiplication facts are here and they start thinking in the families of the Threes, Sixes, Eights, etc.

There is even **a pattern way to learn a 20 X 20 times table** in the back of the book. Students will have to learn a traditional or lattice technique to multiply 2 digit or larger numbers. They are learning to use it quickly and to double-check their answers by reversing the problems (6 X 8 gives the same result as 8 X 6). **Finding the same answer in two different ways on a chart that they made is very satisfying for many students.**

There is a huge amount of information on this Table and it is useful for students to look at similarities, patterns, and go back and forth between addition and multiplication with the Table. They can visually see where the same numbers have more than one factor (24 has half of the numbers 1-10 as factors: 1, 3, 4, 6, and 8).

For 6 X 5= 30, the student can count down 6 Fives, or go down the Ones column to 6 and then over to the Fives column. They have found the answer 30 in two ways. This also **reinforces that multiplication is just adding the same number over and over again.**

Numbers start making more sense to the student. Four 4's and two 8's both add up to 16. They can **SEE** number relationships. They trust the **TREES of the Ones and Twos column** to know that their answers are correct. They can visually see the answers. These TREES of the Ones and Twos can help them learn the multiplication tables by heart because it is not blind memory. The numbers make sense and relate to each other. Studying the numbers with the Table that they created **helps them own the numbers**.

The following **worksheet** gives students an opportunity to expand the use of the EZ Times Table.

2 X 3 =

6 x 2 =

3 x 4 =

4 x 5 =

5 x 6 =

6 x 7 =

7 x 8 =

8 x 9 =

9 x 9 =

9 x 7 =

8 x 6 =

7 x 5 =

6 x 4 =

5 x 3 =

8 x 4 =

7 x 3 =

6 X 9 =

26 / 2 =

24 / 6 =

32 / 8 =

35 / 5 =

63 / 9 =

18 / 4 =

21 / 3 =

49 / 7 =

$$34 \\ \underline{\times 2}$$

$$23 \\ \underline{\times 3}$$

$$35 \\ \underline{\times 4}$$

$$68 \\ \underline{\times 5}$$

$$44 \\ \underline{\times 62}$$

$$73 \\ \underline{\times 96}$$

$$853 \\ \underline{\times 421}$$

Half of 26 is _____

Half of 50 is _____

Half of $88 is _____

Double 4 is _____

Double 7 is _____

Double 8 is _____

Double 16 is _____

Double 25 cents _____

½ of 26 is _____

½ of $38 is _____

½ of $55 is _____

¼ of 20 is _____

¾ of 20 is _____

1/9 of 36 is _____

2/9 of 36 is _____

3/9 of 36 is _____

1/3 of 27 is _____

3 3's are _____

4 4's are _____

5 x 5 is _____

6 squared is _____

7 squared is _____

8^2 is _____

9^2 is _____

Using EZ Times Table in a Home or in the Classroom

The EZTT can be used many ways with a single student or a classroom. To introduce it to a group of students, I recommend use of an overhead projector. **Make a transparency of the blank EZTT** and talk the class through it as you create your own Table on the transparency. Some students often quickly get excited by seeing and creating the patterns. This becomes an incentive for other students to join in the fun. I recommend grouping students who start going ahead ("All students who have finished the Threes already should come over here and do these problems").

Another approach is eliminating the small x1, x2, x3, x4, etc. for the whole class and then giving it to the faster students to fill in. Leaving it out makes the Table easier and clearer for some students, and it is still fully functional. The students just need to count down the numbers in the pattern to multiply and divide (for example, look at 24, find the 6 in the same row, and count down to find that it is the 4th 6 in the Sixes column).

A third addition for fast students is to have them convert their **EZTT** to an **EZ Facts Table** by changing the patterns to the multiplication facts (found in the Ones and Twos columns). The second 6 is erased and replaced with a 12 (which is in the same row in the Twos column). The third 6 is replaced by 18 (in the same row in the Twos column), etc. Have these students replace all patterns with numbers from the same row in the Twos column for the Threes, Fours, Sixes, and Eights columns or give them the **EZ Fill-in Facts** Table.

Students can use their own **EZTT** to work on their math problems for addition, subtraction, multiplication and division for their daily work. Students have chosen to laminate their **EZTT** because it was so valuable to them. They have made their own calculator!

The students could re-create the EZTT once a week. If they use graph paper, they start seeing that they are creating the whole times table "from scratch", which they can do for standarized tests. Even just re-creating the Nines or Sevens in a few seconds on the side of a paper can eliminate errors and build trust.

I highly recommend *Teach Your Child the Multiplication Tables: Fast, Fun & Easy with Dazzling Patterns, Grids & Tricks!* by Eugenia Francis who has created great worksheets that focus on patterns. Please send me ideas and suggestions that I can pass on to other teachers.

Lesson Plan for EZ Times Table

Lesson Plan: EZ Times Table

Combine Goals, Objectives, and Activities that are appropriate for your students. Some of the 3rd, 4th, and 5th grade activities are found in the advanced Part 3.

Time: varies (usually one hour)

Subject: Math

Goals: (Use these California Standards or from your own state)

1st Grade California Standards
1.0 Students understand and use numbers up to 100.
2.0 Students demonstrate the meaning of addition and subtraction and use these operations to solve problems.

2ND Grade California Standards
1.0 Students model, represent, and interpret number relationships to create and solve problems involving addition and subtraction.
3.0 Students model and solve simple problems involving multiplication and division:

3rd Grade California Standards
2.0 Students calculate and solve problems involving addition, subtraction, multiplication, and division:
2.3 Use the inverse relationship of multiplication and division to compute and check results.
2.6 Understand the special properties of 0 and 1 in multiplication and division.

4th Grade California Standards
2.0 Students use two-dimensional coordinate grids to represent points and graph lines and simple figures.
3.0 Students solve problems involving addition, subtraction, multiplication, and division of whole numbers and understand the relationships among the operations.
4.0 Students know how to factor small whole numbers.

5th Grade California Standards
2.0 Students perform calculations and solve problems involving addition, subtraction, and simple multiplication and division of fractions and decimals.
2.0 Students use strategies, skills and concepts in finding solutions.
3.0 Students move beyond a particular problem by generalizing to other situations.

<u>Objectives</u> 1ˢᵗ GRADE: Student will be able to

- ✓ 1.1 ...count, read, and write whole numbers to 100. ... create the Twos from patterns to 64 and beyond.
- ✓ 1.3 ...represent equivalent forms of the same number through the use of physical models, diagrams, and number expressions (to 20) (e.g., 8 may be represented as 4 + 4, 5 + 3, 2 + 2 + 2 + 2, 10 - 2, 11 - 3).
- ✓ ... half or double any number to 32 and beyond.
- ✓ ... add any three numbers from 1-10 in any order resulting in the same answer.
- ✓ ... subtract a smaller number from any number up to 32.

2ᴺᴰ GRADE: Student will be able to:

- ...use repeated addition, arrays, counting by multiples to do multiplying
- ✓ ...Use the commutative and associative rules to simplify mental calculations and to check results.
- ✓ ...Recognize, describe, and extend patterns and determine a next term in linear patterns.
- ✓ Solve problems involving simple number patterns.

3rd GRADE: Student will be able to:

- ✓ ... Recognize and use the commutative and associative properties of multiplication (e.g., if 5 x 7 = 35, then what is 7 x 5?, if 5 x 7 x 3 = 105, then what is 7 x 3 x 5?).
- ✓ ...Use the inverse relationship of multiplication and division to compute and check results.
- ✓ ... Understand the special properties of 0 and 1 in multiplication and division.
- ✓ ... Select appropriate operational and relational symbols to make an expression true (e.g., 4 ___ 3 = 12, what operation symbol goes in the blank?).
- ✓ Use a variety of methods, such as words, numbers, symbols, charts, graphs, tables, diagrams, and models, to explain mathematical reasoning.

4ᵗʰ GRADE: Student will be able to:

- ✓ ... Understand that many whole numbers break down in different ways (e.g., 12 = 4 x 3 = 2 x 6 = 2 x 2 x 3).
- ✓ ...Know that numbers such as 2, 3, 5, 7, and 11 do not have any factors except 1 and themselves and that such numbers are called prime numbers.
- ✓ ...Draw the points corresponding to linear relationships on graph paper.
- ✓ ...Use a variety of methods, such as words, numbers, symbols, charts, graphs, tables, diagrams, and models, to explain mathematical reasoning.

5ᵗʰ GRADE: Student will be able to:

- ✓ 1.4... Determine the prime factors of all numbers through 50.
- ✓ 1.1... Use information taken from a graph or equation to answer questions about a problem situation.
- ✓ 2.3... Use a variety of methods, such as words, numbers, symbols, charts, graphs, tables, and models, to explain mathematical reasoning.

<u>Activities</u>

You may go in sequence or choose whatever the student or class is ready to learn.

Kindergarden
p.8: Create the Ones Number line.

First Grade, EZ Times Table
   p.11: Do addition problems, adding two or more numbers.
   p. 11: Do subtraction problems with EZTT.
   p.12: Create the 2's. Count by 2's,   Double a number, Multiply by 2.
   p. 14 Learn to Divide by 2, to find half of a number.

Second Grade, Ez Times Table
   p. 4-40 Create the EZ Times Table.
   p. 68: Create the Color EZTT.
   p. 37: Add multiples of 1-10 (preparation for multiplication).

Third Grade, EZ Times Table
   p. 43: Multiplication with EZTT.
   p. 60: Create EZ Facts Table. Use EZ Facts to memorize multiplication table.
   p. 45: Find and understand factors on the EZTT.
   p. 55: Threes and Sevens patterns. Fun! See MisterNumbers on Youtube.
   P. 58: Twos, Fours, Sixes, Eights patterns.
   p. 44: Division on the EZTT.
   p. 45: Learn Square Numbers on the EZTT.
   p. 74: Create a Ruler EZTT
   p. 4-40: Create the EZTT on graph paper.

Fourth Grade, EZTT
   p. 56: Learn Rule of Tens.
   p. 70: Create 10 X 10 and 10 X 20 Multiplication Table
   p. 64: Create Time Line Table.
   P. 64: Find factors on Time Line Table.

Fourth & Fifth Grade, EZTT
   p. 72: Create a 20 X 20 Multiplication Table.
   p. 66: Create the Slope Line Table.
   p. 66: Anchor slope lines in Graphing with slope line table.
   p. 64: Find Prime Numbers on Times Line Table.
   P. 72 : Create a 30 x 30 Table on graph paper.

PART 2:

PATTERN PLAY

PART 2 and **PART 3** could be two more books. I include them for those who are curious for more pattern play.

Check out the videos: http://youtube.com/user/MisterNumbers
and the website: http://EZTimesTable.com

Fun Patterns with the Ones-digits and Tens-digits
Feel free to skip this page. Come back if you want to understand ones-digits.

What are **Ones-digits?** We have already worked with the Ones-digits when we created the Ones, Twos, Nines and Tens columns in the EZTT. They are the numbers to the right of the dotted line, in the Ones place. The **Tens-digits** are the digits in the tens place, the number to the left of the dotted line in these four columns. See below. We will use the Ones-digits and Tens-digits for **more pattern play starting on the next page.**

Note that on the last row of the Tens, the tens-digits reach 10 at 100, we could add another dotted line on the left and have 1 in the hundreds-digits.

The **ONES-DIGITS** are circled below. In the EZTT, we started the Ones and Twos with a pattern in the ones-digits.	The **TENS-DIGITS** are circled below. In the EZTT, we started the Nines and Tens with patterns in the tens-digits.

ONES-DIGITS

1	2	9	10
1	2	0 9	1 0
2	4	1 8	2 0
3	6	2 7	3 0
4	8	3 6	4 0
5	0	4 5	5 0
6	2	5 4	6 0
7	4	6 3	7 0
8	6	7 2	8 0
9	8	8 1	9 0
0	0	9 0	10 0
1	2		
2	4		
3	6		
4	8		
5	0		
6	2		
7	4		
8	6		
9	8		
0	0		
1	2		
2	4		
3	6		
4	8		
5	0		
6	2		
7	4		
8	6		
9	8		
0	0		
1	2		
2	4		

The Ones-digits are on the right side of the dotted line in these four columns from the EZTT. We ended making the Nines with a 0-9 pattern going up and the Tens with zeros. See pages 8, 12, 26, and 32 for making the ones-digits in these columns.

TENS-DIGITS

1	2	9	10
1	2	0	1
2	4	1	2
3	6	2	3
4	8	3	4
5	10	4	5
6	12	5	6
7	14	6	7
8	16	7	8
9	18	8	9
10	20	9	10
11	22		
12	24		
13	26		
14	28		
15	30		
16	32		
17	34		
18	36		
19	38		
20	40		
21	42		
22	44		
23	46		
24	48		
25	50		
26	52		
27	54		
28	56		
29	58		
30	60		
31	62		
32	64		

The Tens-digits are on the left side of the dotted line in these four columns from the EZTT. See pages 12, 14, 26 and 30 for making the tens-digits in these columns.

Creating the Threes and Sevens from Patterns: WOW!

The Threes

Make a **Tic-Tac-Toe Square**.

Add the **1-2-3-4-5-6-7-8-9-0** pattern starting from lower left going up. These are **ones-digits**.

3	6	9
2	5	8
1	4	7

0

Add 1's in the Tens-digit place in the second row, and 2's in the third row. You are creating the Threes (3x1 – 3x9).

03	06	09
12	15	18
21	24	27

3x10 = 30

Repeat Tic-Tac-Toe square & 123456789 pattern. Add 3's, 4's, and 5's in each of the next three rows, creating 3x11 – 3 x 19.

33	36	39
42	45	48
51	54	57

3x20 = 60

Repeat Tic-Tac-Toe square & 123456789 pattern. Add 6's, 7's, and 8's in each of the next three rows, creating 3x21 – 3 x 29.

63	66	69
72	75	78
81	84	87

3x30 = 90

Notice that each Tic-ac-Toe square ends with 30, 60, 90, 120, 150…These are threes (3, 6, 9, 12, 15…) with a 0 after it.

3	6	9
2	5	8
1	4	7

3x40 = 120

Continue creating the Threes as long as you like in this fun way.

See MisterNumbers on Youtube for a video.

3	6	9
2	5	8
1	4	7

3x50 = 150

The Sevens

Make a **Tic-Tac-Toe Square**.

Add the **1-2-3-4-5-6-7-8-9-0** pattern starting from upper right and going down. This is the same, but opposite pattern as 3's.

7	4	1
8	5	2
9	6	3

0

As you go across, add 1 to the tens-digit in 2nd & 3rd columns (X's). You are creating the Sevens (7x1 – 7x9).

	X	X
07	14	21
28	35	42
49	56	63

7x10 = 70

Add 70 as the 10th 7. Repeat Tic-Tac-Toe square & 123456789 pattern. Continue to add 1 to the tens-digit in 2nd & 3rd columns (X's) as you go across

	X	X
77	84	91
98	105	112
119	126	133

7x20 = 140

Repeat Tic-Tac-Toe lines and123456789 pattern.

	X	X
7	4	1
8	5	2
9	6	3

7x30 = 210

Notice that each Tic-ac-Toe square ends with 70, 140, 210, 280, 350…These are sevens (7, 14, 21, 28, 35…) with a 0 after it:

	X	X
7	4	1
8	5	2
9	6	3

7x40 = 280

Continue creating the Sevens as long as you like or start over in the last three Squares.

	X	X
7	4	1
8	5	2
9	6	3

Notice on both Threes and Sevens squares that all opposite digits add up to **10: 7+3, 4+6, 1+9, & 2+8.**

7x50 = 350

"RULE OF TENS" PATTERNS

My **Rule of Tens** states that all columns adding up to ten have reversed patterns in the **ones-digits**. Looking just at the ones-digits give us a great place **to explore patterns** in numbers. You just learned used two of them in the Threes and Sevens page. If you understand ones-digits, feel free to **TURN THE PAGE NOW AND CONTINUE TO HAVE FUN** with the Twos, Fours, Sixes, Eights, and creating a 20 X 20 EZ Table from patterns. When you want to know more about **HOW** it works, read this page.

We know that the ones-digit (Could Ones-ie be a simpler name?) holds the ones place, the last digit in a whole number. In the Ones, Twos, Nines and Tens columns, we saw that it is the number to the right of the dotted line, and the **tens-digit** (Tens-ie?) is the digit in the tens place, the number to the left of the dotted line.

All multiplication table ones-digits fall into just 6 patterns (some are reversed). This gets more interesting when one of the patterns is made up **only of Zeros** in the Zero and Tens columns. The Fives end with **alternating 5's and 0's,** and suddenly we are down to only four patterns in the ones-digits. All patterns start and end with 0. We can leave the starting or ending Zero off to see the reverse pattern clearer.

In the EZ Table, we created the ones-digits for both the **Ones and Nines** and they (1 and 9) add up to ten, so let us look at the Rule of Tens. We made the ones-digits for the Ones column with a repeating **0-1-2-3-4-5-6-7-8-9-0**. We created the second half of the Nines with the same pattern. We reversed them by starting at the bottom. So reading **down** the right side of the Nines column is the reverse **0-9-8-7-6-5-4-3-2-1-0**. Look at the 10 x 20 EZ Table on page 74 (where we separate all the ones-digits with a dotted line for 20 rows) for confirmation that the pattern repeats. This is the **third pattern**.

We created the ones-digits for the **Twos** with a repeating **0-2-4-6-8-0** on the right side of the dotted line. By my Rule of Ten, the **Eights** should have the opposite pattern. If we look at the 10 x 20 EZ Table again, we see that, indeed, the Eights pattern is **0-8-6-4-2-0**. This is the **fourth pattern**, which is really a 5-digit pattern when we leave off one of the zeros.

By the Rule of Tens, The **Fours and Sixes** columns should have reversed patterns. We can look at the EZ Facts Table (page 57) to confirm that the ones-digit repeating pattern for the Fours is **4-8-2-6-0** and the Sixes pattern is the opposite, **6-2-8-4-0** (leaving the starting zeros off gives us the 5 repeating numbers). This is the **fifth pattern**.

Our **sixth and last pattern** is in the **Threes** and, by the rule of Tens, the **Sevens** columns (3 + 7 = 10). Looking at the EZ facts Table or the 10 x 20 EZ Table we can see that the patterns for the Threes is **3-6-9-2-5-8-1-4-7-0** and the Sevens have the reverse pattern of **7-4-1-8-5-2-6-3-1-0**. We have seen in the Threes and Sevens page this easy way to visualize these patterns in sets of Three on a **Tic-tac-Toe square,** with the zero below. Threes add 3 to 3, 2, 1 while the Sevens subtract 3 from 7, 8, 9.

Threes: 3-6-9, 2-5-8, 1-4-7, 0   **Sevens:** 7-4-1, 8-5-2, 9-6-3, 0

3	6	9
2	5	8
1	4	7

0

7	4	1
8	5	2
9	6	3

0

The Six patterns and their opposites in the Ones-digits

All patterns start and end in Zero, the starting zero has been left off.

Column	Repeating Pattern & Reverse	Also shows up in larger Table
For Zeros	0-0	Tens, Twenties, ...
For Fives	5-0	Fifteens, Twentyfives, ...
For Ones	1-2-3-4-5-6-7-8-9-0	Elevens, Twenty-ones, ...
For Nines	9-8-7-6-5-4-3-2-1-0 (reverse)	Nineteens, Twenty-nines, ...
For Twos	2-4-6-8-0	Twelves, Twenty-twos, ...
For Eights	8-6-4-2-0 (reverse of Twos)	Eighteens, Twenty-eights, ...
For Fours	4-8-2-6-0	Fourteens, Twenty-fours, ...
For Sixes	6-2-8-4-0 (reverse of Fours)	Sixteens, Twenty-sixes, ...
For Threes	3-6-9-2-5-8-1-4-7-0	Thirteens, Twenty-Threes, ...
For Sevens	7-4-1-8-5-2-7-4-1-0 (reverse)	Seventeens, Twenty-sevens, ..

If we look at the 20 x 20 EZ Table on page 72, we see that the patterns in the ones-digits are the same for 1 and 11, 2 and 12, 3 and 13, 4 and 14, 5 and 15... If we make the Table even wider, we will see that all numbers ending in 1 will repeat the **1-2-3-4-5-6-7-8-9-0** pattern, all numbers ending in 2 will repeat the **2-4-6-8-0** pattern, all numbers ending in 4 will repeat the **4-8-2-6-0** pattern, numbers ending in 5 will repeat the **5-0** pattern, and so forth.

You will now use these patterns to create the Twos, Fours, Sixes, and Eights, and you can use these patterns in **Part 3** to create several multiplication tables.

Patterns for the Twos, Fours, Sixes and Eights

We will create these times tables from patterns in groups of 5 repeating numbers in 5 columns. The Twos and Eights, as well as the Fours and Sixes, have the same but opposite sequence in the first four numbers of the Ones-digits and end in 0. **If a ones-digit in a box below is less than the one to its left, it has an X above it**. Since it is less, **we increase the Tens-digit by one** (We are "carrying" a ten when we pass 0). Once we establish where the X's are, we can fill in the tens-digits. The left tables show the pattern, then adds the tens-digits. The right column is for you.

The Twos repeating pattern in the ones-digits is **24680**. Only 0 is less than the number to its left (8) and has an X above it. So at 0, the tens-digit always increases by 1. On the left table we add a 1 in front of the first 0. Continue with 1's in the second row until the 0 gets a 2. We are creating the Twos with this pattern. Continue to create the Twos on the right table.

Create the Twos pattern X

2	4	6	8	0
2	4	6	8	0
2	4	6	8	0

Add the tens-digits X

2	4	6	8	10
12	14	16	18	20
22	24	26	28	30

Create your own Twos X

2	4	6	8	0
2	4	6	8	0
2	4	6	8	0
2	4	6	8	0
2	4	6	8	0
2	4	6	8	0
2	4	6	8	0
2	4	6	8	0

The Eights repeating pattern is the **opposite** (putting the zero last): **86420**. The 6, 4, 2, and 0 are decreasing and get an X above their columns. This means that their tens-digits increase by one. So in each row, we add 1 under each X to make multiplication by 8. The 0 column makes **8** x5, x10, x15... Multiplying by 8 the EZ way!

Create the Eights Pattern

	X	X	X	X
8	6	4	2	0
8	6	4	2	0
8	6	4	2	0

Add the tens-digits

	X	X	X	X
8	16	24	32	40
48	56	64	72	80
88	96	104	112	120

Create your own Eights

	X	X	X	X
8	6	4	2	0
8	6	4	2	0
8	6	4	2	0
8	6	4	2	0
8	6	4	2	0
8	6	4	2	0
8	6	4	2	0
8	6	4	2	0

The Fours repeating pattern is **48260**. The 2 and 0 are getting smaller and get an X above their columns. This means that their tens-digits increase by one. In the first row, we add 1 & 2 under the X's to create 4,8,12,16,& 20. Say aloud the rhythm of the tens-digits:22334, 44556, …

Create the Fours Pattern

		X		X
4	8	2	6	0
4	8	2	6	0
4	8	2	6	0

Add the tens-digits

		X		X
4	8	12	16	20
24	28	32	36	40
44	48	52	56	60

Create your own 4's

		X		X
4	8	2	6	0
4	8	2	6	0
4	8	2	6	0
4	8	2	6	0
4	8	2	6	0
4	8	2	6	0
4	8	2	6	0
4	8	2	6	0

The Sixes repeating pattern is **62840**, **opposite** of the Fours. The 2, 4, and 0 are getting smaller and get an X above their columns. This means that their tens-digits increase by one. In the first row, we add 1's under the X's to create 6 x 5 =30. The next rows end in 60 & 90. Isn't this **fun** and amazing? See MisterNumbers on Youtube.

Create the Sixes Pattern

	X		X	X
6	2	8	4	0
6	2	8	4	0
6	2	8	4	0

Add the tens-digits

	X		X	X
6	12	18	24	30
36	42	48	54	60
66	72	78	84	90

Create your own 6's

	X		X	X
6	2	8	4	0
6	2	8	4	0
6	2	8	4	0
6	2	8	4	0
6	2	8	4	0
6	2	8	4	0
6	2	8	4	0
6	2	8	4	0

PART 3:

ADVANCED EZ TABLES

The first advanced table is the **_EZ Facts Table_**, which is helpful to almost all students.

We have created most of the times table in two ways. First we created the EZ Times Table and then we created the Threes, Sevens, Twos, Fours, Sixes and Eights from patterns. Now we can create a 20 x 20 times table purely from patterns. Those who play here often feel that numbers are fun and friendly.

EZ FACTS Table

This important Table is an **EZ FACTS Table**, where the patterns are replaced by the actual numbers in the Three, Four, Six and Eight columns. It is included with the EZTT because students can use this table to **see and memorize the times table facts** in relation to each other.

It is identical in structure to the original EZTT, but adds a way to see each multiplication fact and how it fits within its own family and with other columns too. This Table focuses on the actual numbers in the Threes, Fours, Sixes and Eights. Directions for creating this Table are on the next page.

The students can be encouraged to count by Ones, Twos, Threes, Fours, Fives, Sixes, Sevens, Eights, Nines, and Tens while looking at the Table and then without looking at the Table.

When a young student counts beyond ten, they sometimes lose a grasp of the numbers. The Table gives them a count by Ones up to 32 in boxes that are countable, evenly spaced, and give a sense of scale. Right next to it is a double scale (the Twos) counting in even numbers to 64. With the Ones next to it, numbers up to 64 are now grounded in a reality accepted by the student. Counting by Twos is familiar and the student can go back and forth with the Ones and Twos to **double any number or half any number** (12 + 12 = 24, 13 X 2 = 26, ½ of 28 = 14, 30 / 2 = 15).

Counting down by Threes is easy to visualize because they are next to, and identical to the Ones. This makes sense to the student.

The even numbers are condensed scales so that jumps of 4, 6, and 8 become jumps of 2, 3, and 4, which are much easier and more friendly.

Each student sees different patterns when they look at this Table. The same numbers that make up the times table keep showing up again and again in meaningful ways. Notice that 24 in the Twos column, and that 24 in the Fours, the Sixes, the Eights columns. There is also a 24 in the Threes column next to the 24 in the Ones column. There are also 48's across the column. Every other 4 is an Eight. The Sixes are in the same row as the Threes and each Three is doubled in the Sixes. What else do you see?

EZ TIMES TABLE

9	7	5	3	1	2	4	6	8	10
Odd Numbers						Even Numbers			
0 9	7	5	•	1	2	•	•	•	1 0
1 8	14	10	•	2	4	4 x1	•	•	2 0
2 7	21	15	3 x1	3	6	•	6 x1	•	3 0
3 6	28	20	•	4	8	4 x2	•	8 x1	4 0
4 5	35	25	•	5	10	•	•	•	5 0
5 4	42	30	3 x2	6	12	4 x3	6 x2	•	6 0
6 3	49	35	•	7	14	•	•	•	7 0
7 2	56	40	•	8	16	4 x4	•	8 x2	8 0
8 1	63	45	3 x3	9	18	•	6 x3	•	9 0
9 0	70	50	•	10	20	4 x5	•	•	10 0
			•	11	22	•	•	•	
			3 x4	12	24	4 x6	6 x4	8 x3	
			•	13	26	•	•	•	
			•	14	28	4 x7	•	•	
			3 x5	15	30	•	6 x5	•	
			•	16	32	4 x8	•	8 x4	
			•	17	34	•	•	•	
			3 x6	18	36	4 x9	6 x6	•	
			•	19	38	•	•	•	
			•	20	40	4 x10	•	8 x5	
			3 x7	21	42	•	6 x7	•	
			•	22	44	4	•	•	
			•	23	46	•	•	•	
			3 x8	24	48	4	6 x8	8 x6	
			•	25	50	•	•	•	
			•	26	52	4	•	•	
			3 x9	27	54	•	6 x9	•	
			•	28	56	4	•	8 x7	
			•	29	58	•	•	•	
			3 x10	30	60	4	6 x10	•	
			•	31	62	•	•	•	
			•	32	64	4	•	8 x8	

Use the Ones column to multiply the Fives, Sevens, Nines, and Tens.

0 X any number = 0

The Zeros Table copyright©Thomas Biesanz www.eztimestable.com

EZ FILL-IN FACTS Table

Students who have created an EZ Times Table can form the **Facts Table** on the previous page. One way is to erase the 3's in the Threes column, replacing them with numbers from the Ones column. They can create the Fours, Sixes, and Eights in the same manner by erasing and filling in the numbers from the Twos column.

The table on the right is an exercise for students who understand the EZ Times Table to quickly **create the FACTS Table** on the previous page. Creating the Fill-In Facts chart allows them to keep their original **EZTT** that they value and create the Facts Table too. The need for erasing on the EZTT is eliminated. Fun and neat.

They now have the sets of the Ones, Twos, Threes, Fours, Fives, Sixes, Seven, Eights, Nines, and Tens. Each is still in the structure of the EZ Times Table and the relationship to the Ones and Twos are still evident. Now they can easily memorize the facts from a chart that they made. Creating this chart makes it easier to move up or down one or two boxes to figure out any facts they are unsure of. **They have the structure of each set of numbers.**

They have accepted the Ones and Twos as accurate and the dot patterns are already in place in the Threes, Fours, Sixes, and Eights columns. Even the little "x1, x2,..." are in place in the openings in the dot pattern on the table on the right.

The student creates the Threes by going down to each open box in the pattern, seeing the number in the same row of the Ones, and putting in that number in the Ones column. So the first open box (cell) in the Threes column (. . _) is a 3. At the next open box, the student puts a 6 since it is in the same row of the Ones. The third box is a 9, and down they go to 30. They have now created the set of the Threes.

They also create the Fours (4, 8, 12, 16,...), Sixes (6, 12, 18, 24, ...) and Eights (8, 16, 24, 32...) in a similar manner by pulling numbers from the Twos column. They have created the sets of the Fours, Sixes and Eights. This allows them to see each of these sets separate, but connected to the Ones and Twos.

They again re-create the Tens, Fives, Nines, and Tens similar to the EZ Times Table. Notice that one **factor** for each number found on the Table is the column that contains it. The other factor is the little number next to the x, or it is the number in the Ones column. For example, we find 18 in the Sixes Column and it has a x3 behind it which means that 6 and 3 are factors. 15 is in the Fives column in the same row as 3 in the Ones column and so 5 and 3 are factors.

EZ TIMES TABLE

9	7	5	3	1	2	4	6	8	10
			Odd Numbers			Even Numbers			
			•	1	2	•	•	•	
			•	2	4	x1	•	•	
			x1	3	6	•	x1	•	
			•	4	8	x2	•	x1	
			•	5	10	•	•	•	
			x2	6	12	x3	x2	•	
		☐	•	7	14	•	•	•	
			•	8	16	x4	•	x2	
			x3	9	18	•	x3	•	
			•	10	20	x5	•	•	
			•	11	22	•	•	•	
			x4	12	24	x6	x4	x3	
			•	13	26	•	•	•	
			•	14	28	x7	•	•	
			x5	15	30	•	x5	•	
			•	16	32	x8	•	x4	
			•	17	34	•	•	•	
			x6	18	36	x9	x6	•	
			•	19	38	•	•	•	
			•	20	40	x10	•	x5	
			x7	21	42	•	x7	•	
			•	22	44		•	•	
			•	23	46	•	•	•	
			x8	24	48		x8	x6	
			•	25	50	•	•	•	
			•	26	52		•	•	
			x9	27	54	•	x9	•	
			•	28	56		•	x7	
			•	29	58	•	•	•	
			x10	30	60		x10	•	
			•	31	62	•	•	•	
			•	32	64		•	x8	

Use the Ones column to multiply the Fives, Sevens, Nines, and Tens.

Zero X any number = zero   Fill In EZ Table copyright2008©Tom Biesanz NumbersREZ@aol.com

VARIATIONS OF THE EZ TIMES TABLES

The EZ Times Table (EZTT) that the student has already created contains the whole multiplication table. They are hooked. There is nothing weird or scary about it. They count by Ones and Twos, count up to three, and do their Fives. Everything else falls into place in a way that they totally understand. Viewing the Table in different forms can facilitate fun understanding and learning math the easy way. A **Color EZ Times Table** can be created using different colors for each number.

THE TIMES LINE TABLE

The **Times Line Table** on the right uses the dots pattern from the **EZTT**. The Ones and Twos columns increase to 50 rows and are still the anchors of the table. The main difference is that 5, 7, 9, and 10 are also done as dot patterns. A student sees that Fives can also be dot, dot, dot, dot, 5, and similar patterns can be created for the Sevens, Nines and Tens. **The numbers arrange themselves in angle line patterns.** The lines of these patterns are drawn on this table and we can see that the first lines are all multiplication-times-one problems for the even and the odd numbers.

The first 9 is in the same row in the Nines column as it is in the Ones column, and the 3, 5, and 7 that are in the same line are also repeated in the Ones column. In the 2X line on the even side, the second 10 is in the same row as the 20 in the Twos column (10 X 2= 20). Look at the 4X (multiplication-by-4) line on the left and find the 7. Looking in the same row in the Ones column, we find the answer, 28. **Similar results are found for every number on a line.** Students can accurately guess that **all whole numbers are on lines if the chart is long enough.**

Prime numbers show up on this chart (see page 44). Numbers outside the Ones and Twos column indicate **factors** in the same row. The numbers without factors (only dots) in their rows are circled and are **prime numbers**. We could continue the chart and have students **find more prime numbers**.

This table can be created by students on graph paper for a "**Wow**" learning experience. Use large square graph paper and use ten squares width, or for more rows, use small square graph paper and use two square width for each column.

VARIATIONS ON THE FOLLOWING PAGES

This is followed in the next pages by the **Slope Lines Table** which is very similar with an amazing twist for graph charts, **Patterns create an *EZ 20 x 20 Table*** and an **EZ Ruler Table** making the times table on a blank sheet.

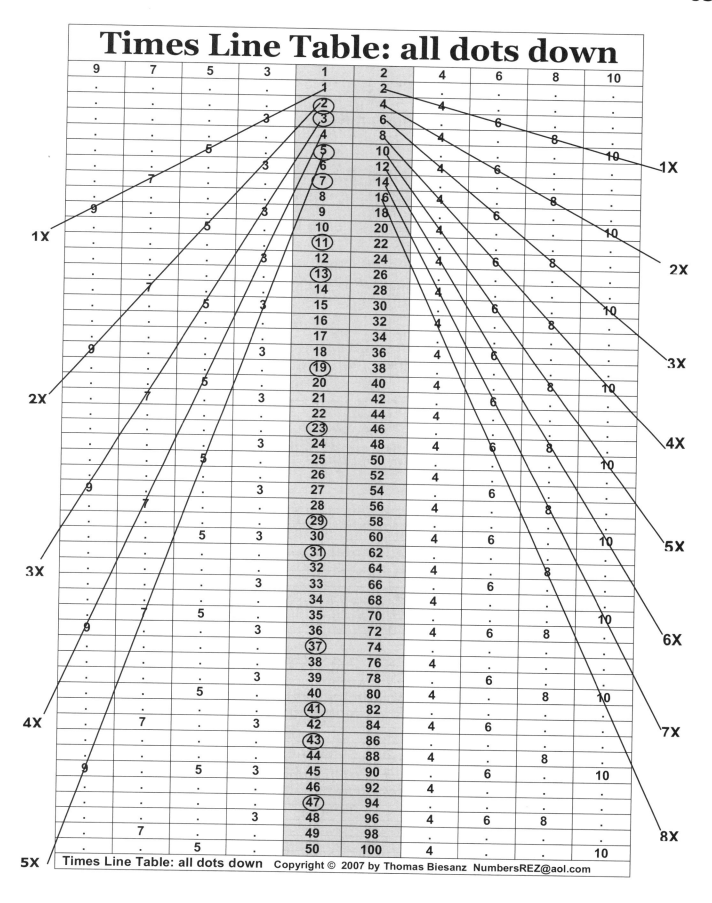

Times Line Table: all dots down

MORE VARIATIONS ON THE NEXT PAGES

The **Times Line Table** is followed in the next pages by the **Slope Lines Table** which is very similar with an amazing twist for graph charts, Patterns creating an **EZ 20 x 20 Table**, and **an EZ Ruler Table** that creates the times table on a blank sheet.

THE SLOPE LINE TABLE

The *Slope Line Table* on the right is fascinating to many students when they see the patterns that the numbers create. It is identical to the *Times Line Table* except the numbers start at the bottom and the boxes are square. The first line at the bottom is the One times line. (One times the number is the same number). The second line is the 2X line (2 x 4 = 8, 2 x 6 = 12...). The third and fourth lines are the 3x and 4x lines (3 or 4 times the number is found in the Twos column). This is similar to the *Times Line* table.

What is amazing is that the **One-times-line (1x)**, looking at the table as a graph, is also **the slope line y=1x**. The Two times line (2x) is the slope line y=2X. This gives students similar results for y=3x, y= 4x... Students now have a memory anchor for the angle of different slope lines.

Now students can look at a y=1x slope line and see a practical form that it takes that is real to them, that they created. They can remember that as the value of X gets larger, the slope line gets sharper, just as you multiply by a larger number, the number increases.

THE COLOR EZ TIMES TABLE

A fun color Table can be created with different colors for each number. This gives a nice graphic picture of how the different numbers relate. Making the **EZTT** in color is a **right-brain way** for students to help the number families come alive and make the Table visually appealing. This can be expanded to the EZ Facts table, adding colors for factors of the number.

THE IMPORTANCE OF PATTERN RECOGNITION

Kids notice patterns with all the Tables, like the Threes and Sixes are in the same rows, and that every other 4 is an 8, and that the Eights end with a repeated 8, 6, 4, 2, 0 pattern. Students love the dot patterns and these patterns include numbers, and soon the numbers are easier. An older friend told me he was recruited to do early computer programming based, not on math ability, but on pattern recognition. The variations of the EZ Times Table all teach pattern recognition. Right-brain creative insights and learnings in life and in school are based on noticing patterns and seeing relationships.

Slope Lines Table

All-Dots, going up
© 2007 Thomas Biesanz
www.eztimestable.com

Y = 4 X

Y = 3 X

Y = 2 X

Y = 1 X

9	7	5	3	1	2	4	6	8	10
				29	58				
	7			28	56	4		8	
9			3	27	54		6		
				26	52	4			
		5		25	50				10
			3	24	48	4	6	8	
				23	46				
				22	44	4			
	7		3	21	42		6		
		5		20	40	4		8	10
				19	38				
9			3	18	36	4	6		
				17	34				
				16	32	4		8	
		5	3	15	30		6		10
	7			14	28	4			
				13	26				
			3	12	24	4	6	8	
				11	22				
		5		10	20	4			10
9			3	9	18		6		
				8	16	4		8	
	7			7	14				
			3	6	12	4	6		
		5		5	10				10
				4	8	4		8	
			3	3	6		6		
				2	4	4			
				1	2				
9	7	5	3	1	2	4	6	8	10

Slope Line Table   copyright 2007 Thomas Biesanz

NUMBER PATTERNS 10 x 10

From this page to the end of the book **is extra** for those students who enjoy seeing and playing with the patterns. In the top table on the next page, all ten columns are divided by dotted lines like the Ones, Twos, Nines and Tens were in the EZTT. These four columns are copied here and the numbers for the Threes, Fours, Sixes, and Eights are found in the **EZTT** or in the **EZFT** (EZ Facts Table). They are placed here with the dotted lines separating the the **ones-digits** (the single number to the right) and the **tens-digits.**

A learning progression is to have students create the **EZTT** with verbal instructions and use of an overhead projector, then create the **EZTT** on their own, then create the **EZ Facts Table,** and then this **EZ 10 x 10 Table.** Each step helps the student see the fun patterns while learning the multiplication facts. **This results in a form of the EZTT that is similar in some ways to a standard times table,** but we have established patterns that we can continue to play with to see how full of fun patterns numbers can be.

NUMBER PATTERNS 10 x 20

The lower table is identical to the upper table, but is extended down to 20 rows. The Ones and Twos are already done past 20 rows in the **EZTT** and can be transferred to the empty table. The Ones can be put in the left column of the Tens and finished by putting zeros in the ones-digit column.

The ones-digits: Look at the EZTT and see that the ones-digit patterns repeat for every number (except that 3, 7 and 9 have ended in 0 and are ready to repeat). The dotted lines again divide each column into ones and tens columns. Repeat ones-digit patterns in all right columns for 2-9 all the way down the chart. Since 3, 7, and 9 ended in 0, they start over with 3, 7, and 9 in the 11th row and repeat their respective patterns from the **EZTT**.

The Tens digits: We already have the first ten rows for 3-9 in this chart from EZTT. To do the next tens-digit in 3-9, look at the number above on the ones-digit side. If **the new ones digit number is larger, repeat the previous number** on the left. **If it is smaller, increase the number by one**. For example, after 30 (tenth row of the Threes), the pattern indicates a shift from 0 to 3 in the ones-digit. Since the 3 is larger than the 0, the tens-digit remains the same: 33 (11th row). After 39 the ones digit pattern indicates a shift from 9 to 3. Since the 3 is smaller, the tens increase to 4, resulting in 42). Using this pattern works for all columns.

Look at how it works on the EZ Pattern 10 x 20 Table and re-create it using these rules on the empty EZ 20 x 20 Table when you turn the page.

Check MisterNumbers on Youtube.com for help creating this table.

Seeing the Patterns in the Ones-digits and Tens-digits

EZ Patterns 10 x 10 ©2007 Tom Biesanz

9	7	5	3	1	2	4	6	8	10
09	07	5	3	1	2	4	6	8	10
18	14	10	6	2	4	8	12	16	20
27	21	15	9	3	6	12	18	24	30
36	28	20	12	4	8	16	24	32	40
45	35	25	15	5	10	20	30	40	50
54	42	30	18	6	12	24	36	48	60
63	49	35	21	7	14	28	42	56	70
72	56	40	24	8	16	32	48	64	80
81	63	45	27	9	18	36	54	72	90
90	70	50	30	10	20	40	60	80	100

Using the Patterns in the Ones-digits and Tens-digits

EZ Patterns 10 x 20 ©2007 Tom Biesanz

9	7	5	3	1	2	4	6	8	10
09	7	5	3	1	2	4	6	8	10
18	14	10	6	2	4	8	12	16	20
27	21	15	9	3	6	12	18	24	30
36	28	20	12	4	8	16	24	32	40
45	35	25	15	5	10	20	30	40	50
54	42	30	18	6	12	24	36	48	60
63	49	35	21	7	14	28	42	56	70
72	56	40	24	8	16	32	48	64	80
81	63	45	27	9	18	36	54	72	90
90	70	50	30	10	20	40	60	80	100
99	77	55	33	11	22	44	66	88	110
108	84	60	36	12	24	48	72	96	120
117	91	65	39	13	26	52	78	104	130
126	98	70	42	14	28	56	84	112	140
135	105	75	45	15	30	60	90	120	150
144	112	80	48	16	32	64	96	128	160
153	119	85	51	17	34	68	102	136	170
162	126	90	54	18	36	72	108	144	180
171	133	95	57	19	38	76	114	152	190
180	140	100	60	20	40	80	120	160	200

NUMBER PATTERNS TO 20 x 20

The top half of the **EZ 20 x 20 Table** is the **EZ 10 x 20** Table from the previous page. The bottom half is the EZ 11 x 20 patterns. These are lined up so that the Nineteens are located directly below the Nines, The Seventeens are located directly below the Sevens, etc. In the top half, the Ones show you the row numbers. There are numbers on the right to show the row number in the lower half of the Table.

Notice that the ones-digit in the right column have created a pattern in the 10 x 20 top portion of the Table and are exactly the same numbers in the same pattern in the Nines as in the Nineteens. This holds true for every column and **you can fill in all the ones-digits in the Eleven to Nineteen columns simply be repeating the patterns** established in the Ones to Tens columns above them!

See that this is true on the EZ 20 x 20 Table on the right and fill in those patterns on the blank EZ 20 x 20 Table when you turn the page. You may want to use your **EZTT** or the **EZMFT** to see the patterns. You have now created all the ones-digits for the 20 x 20 Table

Now we will use a similar pattern from the last page to create the **tens-digits** on the 11 x 20 part of the table. In the first row of 12-19, put a 1 in the left column to create the numbers 12-19, since the ones-digits are already in place. To do the next row, look at the number above on the ones-digit side.

If the new ones-digit number is larger, increase the previous number on the left by one. If it is smaller, increase the number by two (e.g. after 12, the ones-digit pattern indicates a shift from 2 to 4 in the ones digit. Since the 4 is larger than 2, the tens increase by 1: resulting in 24. After 48 the pattern indicates a shift from 8 to 0. Since the 0 is smaller, the tens increase by two, resulting in 60)**. Use this pattern going down the tens-digit columns** to fill in all the numbers.

You are done. I hope you made it through the maze of words because the patterns are fairly simple and creating the Table is satisfying.

You can actually start with a blank 20 x 20 table, fill in the Ones-digits from the Rule of Tens, and use the two rules for Tens-digits to fill in the whole table. There is also a blank 20 x 20 Table for you to fill in with these patterns. The Ones are filled in as well as the first row of 11-19 to get you started. Follow the instructions on the last pages and you will have created the times table to 20x20 from patterns without doing any multipying!

Creating EZ Patterns 20 x 20 in two parts (10 x 20 and 11 x 20)

EZ Patterns 10 x 20 ©2007 Tom Biesanz

9	7	5	3	1	2	4	6	8	10
0 9	7	5	3	1	2	4	6	8	1 0
1 8	1 4	1 0	6	2	4	8	1 2	1 6	2 0
2 7	2 1	1 5	9	3	6	1 2	1 8	2 4	3 0
3 6	2 8	2 0	1 2	4	8	1 6	2 4	3 2	4 0
4 5	3 5	2 5	1 5	5	1 0	2 0	3 0	4 0	5 0
5 4	4 2	3 0	1 8	6	1 2	2 4	3 6	4 8	6 0
6 3	4 9	3 5	2 1	7	1 4	2 8	4 2	5 6	7 0
7 2	5 6	4 0	2 4	8	1 6	3 2	4 8	6 4	8 0
8 1	6 3	4 5	2 7	9	1 8	3 6	5 4	7 2	9 0
9 0	7 0	5 0	3 0	1 0	2 0	4 0	6 0	8 0	10 0
9 9	7 7	5 5	3 3	1 1	2 2	4 4	6 6	8 8	11 0
10 8	8 4	6 0	3 6	1 2	2 4	4 8	7 2	9 6	12 0
11 7	9 1	6 5	3 9	1 3	2 6	5 2	7 8	10 4	13 0
12 6	9 8	7 0	4 2	1 4	2 8	5 6	8 4	11 2	14 0
13 5	10 5	7 5	4 5	1 5	3 0	6 0	9 0	12 0	15 0
14 4	11 2	8 0	4 8	1 6	3 2	6 4	9 6	12 8	16 0
15 3	11 9	8 5	5 1	1 7	3 4	6 8	10 2	13 6	17 0
16 2	12 6	9 0	5 4	1 8	3 6	7 2	10 8	14 4	18 0
17 1	13 3	9 5	5 7	1 9	3 8	7 6	11 4	15 2	19 0
18 0	14 0	10 0	6 0	2 0	4 0	8 0	12 0	16 0	20 0

EZ Patterns 11 x 20 ©2007 Tom Biesanz

19	17	15	13	11	12	14	16	18	20	
1 9	1 7	1 5	1 3	1 1	1 2	1 4	1 6	1 8	2 0	1
3 8	3 4	3 0	2 6	2 2	2 4	2 8	3 2	3 6	4 0	2
5 7	5 1	4 5	3 9	3 3	3 6	4 2	4 8	5 4	6 0	3
7 6	6 8	6 0	5 2	4 4	4 8	5 6	6 4	7 2	8 0	4
9 5	8 5	7 5	6 5	5 5	6 0	7 0	8 0	9 0	10 0	5
11 4	10 2	9 0	7 8	6 6	7 2	8 4	9 6	10 8	12 0	6
13 3	11 9	10 5	9 1	7 7	8 4	9 8	11 2	12 6	14 0	7
15 2	13 6	12 0	10 4	8 8	9 6	11 2	12 8	14 4	16 0	8
17 1	15 3	13 5	11 7	9 9	10 8	12 6	14 4	16 2	18 0	9
19 0	17 0	15 0	13 0	11 0	12 0	14 0	16 0	18 0	20 0	10
20 9	18 7	16 5	14 3	12 1	13 2	15 4	17 6	19 8	22 0	11
22 8	20 4	18 0	15 6	13 2	14 4	16 8	19 2	21 6	24 0	12
24 7	22 1	19 5	16 9	14 3	15 6	18 2	20 8	23 4	26 0	13
26 6	23 8	21 0	18 2	15 4	16 8	19 6	22 4	25 2	28 0	14
28 5	25 5	22 5	19 5	16 5	18 0	21 0	24 0	27 0	30 0	15
30 4	27 2	24 0	20 8	17 6	19 2	22 4	25 6	28 8	32 0	16
32 3	28 9	25 5	22 1	18 7	20 4	23 8	27 2	30 6	34 0	17
34 2	30 6	27 0	23 4	19 8	21 6	25 2	28 8	32 4	36 0	18
36 1	32 3	28 5	24 7	20 9	22 8	26 6	30 4	34 2	38 0	19
38 0	34 0	30 0	26 0	22 0	24 0	28 0	32 0	36 0	40 0	20

Create your own 20 x 20 Times Table here from Patterns

EZ Patterns in Ones through Tens ©2007 Tom Biesanz

9	7	5	3	1	2	4	6	8	10
				1					
				2					
				3					
				4					
				5					
				6					
				7					
				8					
				9					
				10					
				11					
				12					
				13					
				14					
				15					
				16					
				17					
				18					
				19					
				20					

EZ Patterns in Elevens Through Twenties ©2007 Tom Biesanz

19	17	15	13	11	12	14	16	18	20	
19	17	15	13	11	12	14	16	18	20	1
										2
										3
										4
										5
										6
										7
										8
										9
										10
										11
										12
										13
										14
										15
										16
										17
										18
										19
										20

EZ RULER TABLE

This EZ Ruler Table is created on a blank sheet of paper with just **a 1" wide ruler and a pencil.** It is interesting to view new patterns and **see how the Threes and Sixes, and Fours and Eights are connected.** It is also possible to re-create part or all of it in a testing situation. I suggest doing an **EZTT** first because it will establish how to create the Ones and Twos accurately. Neatness helps and variations are included at the bottom of this page. The next few pages will demonstrate the steps in creating the **EZ Ruler Table**.

1. Put the ruler along the top of the page and draw a line on the lower side.
2. Put the pencil tip roughly in the center of that line and draw a line down the page perpendicular to the first line. Accuracy is not important here.
3. Put the top of the ruler on the horizontal line and draw a line on the lower side of the ruler making a parallel line. Repeat until you have 9 evenly spaced horizontal lines.
4. Put a big 1 above the left side of the T made by the first two lines. Placing four numbers per line, put the numbers 1-32 just to the left of the vertical line.
5. Put a big 2 above the right side of the T made by the first two lines. Using four numbers per line, put the even numbers 2-64 just to the right of the vertical line.
6. Put a small-circled ⟨3 6⟩ above the big 1 and 2. Count every third set of numbers (3 and 6, 6 and 12, 9 and 18, etc.) and enclose with an oval.
7. Put a ▢4 8▢ in a rectangle above the big 1 and 2. Put a rectangle enclosing numbers that are just above the lines. Rectangles create the 4's and 8's. Starting at the vertical line, draw horizontal lines to the left under the 1, 2, 3, 5, 6, 7, 9, and 10 (lines are already under the 4 and 8).
8. Put a big 5 to the left of the big 1. Count by Fives down to 50 in the ten spaces.
9. Put a big 9 to the far left of the big 1. Put a vertical dotted line down the ten spaces. Put 0-9 going down the left side of the dotted line and 0-9 going up the right side of the dotted line. This creates the Nines.
10. Put a big 7 between the big 5 and the big 9. Put 49 in the seventh space.

You are done. Count the circles to multiply by 3 and 6 and count the lines to multiply by 4 and 8. The other numbers are similar to the **EZTT**.

Variations: Use these variations to make the Table neater and give more and faster answers.

1. Use dotted lines for the Ones and Twos column for accuracy.
2. Number the horizontal lines starting with 1 after the first four numbers. This gives the number for multiplication by 4 and 8. The sixth line: 4 x 4 = 16 and 4 x 8 = 32. Also number the ovals for multilplying by 3 and 6.
3. Extending the Ones and Twos to 36 and 72 below the last horizontal line gives more answers.
4. Count down every 5th set of numbers and put an arrow in front of the numbers in the Ones and Twos columns. This creates your Fives and Tens.
5. Create these patterns on the **EZTT** after creating the Ones and Twos. The last Table shows the variations and tips on how to use this Table. Enjoy!

1	2
1	2
2	4
3	6
4	8
5	10
6	12
7	14
8	16
9	18
10	20
11	22
12	24
13	26
14	28
15	30
16	32
17	34
18	36
19	38
20	40
21	42
22	44
23	46
24	48
25	50
26	52
27	54
28	56
29	58
30	60
31	62
32	64

1	2
1	2
2	4
3	6
4	8
5	10
6	12
7	14
8	16
9	18
10	20
11	22
12	24
13	26
14	28
15	30
16	32
17	34
18	36
19	38
20	40
21	42
22	44
23	46
24	48
25	50
26	52
27	54
28	56
29	58
30	60
31	62
32	64

	9	7	5	1	2 (3) (4 8)
0	9		5	1	2
1	8		10	2	4
2	7		15	3	6
3	6		20	4	8
4	5		25	5	10
5	4		30	6	12
6	3	49	35	7	14
7	2		40	8	16
8	1		45	9	18
9	0		50	10	20
				11	22
				12	24
				13	26
				14	28
				15	30
				16	32
				17	34
				18	36
				19	38
				20	40
				21	42
				22	44
				23	46
				24	48
				25	50
				26	52
				27	54
				28	56
				29	58
				30	60
				31	62
				32	64

9		7	5	1	4 / 8	2
0	9		5	1		2
1	8		10	2		4
2	7		15	3		6 (1)
3	6		20	4		8
4	5		25 →	5		1 0
5	4		30	6		1 2 (2)
6	3	49	35	7		1 4
7	2		40	8		1 6
8	1		45	9		1 8 (3)
9	0		50 →	1 0		2 0
				1 1		2 2
				1 2		2 4 (4)
				1 3		2 6
				1 4		2 8
→				1 5		3 0 (5)
				1 6		3 2
				1 7		3 4
				1 8		3 6 (6)
				1 9		3 8
→				2 0		4 0
				2 1		4 2 (7)
				2 2		4 4
				2 3		4 6
				2 4		4 8 (8)
→				2 5		5 0
				2 6		5 2
				2 7		5 4 (9)
				2 8		5 6
				2 9		5 8
→				3 0		6 0 (10)
				3 1		6 2
				3 2		6 4
				3 3		6 6 (11)
				3 4		6 8
→				3 5		7 0
				3 6		7 2

Line numbers (right margin): 1, 2, 3, 4, 5, 6, 7, 8, 9

Callout: This 4th oval on the left shows that the fourth 3 is 12 and the fourth 6 is 24.

Callout: This rectangle on the left and the line number show that the fifth 4 is 20 and the fifth 8 is 40

Callout: The sixth arrow shows that the sixth 5 is 30 and the sixth 10 is 60

Fun Patterns in Numbers

$1 \times 1 = 1$
$11 \times 11 = 121$
$111 \times 111 = 12321$
$1111 \times 1111 = 1234321$
$11111 \times 11111 = 123454321$
$111111 \times 111111 = 12345654321$
$1111111 \times 1111111 = 1234567654321$
$11111111 \times 11111111 = 123456787654321$

$1 \times 9 + 2 = 11$
$12 \times 9 + 3 = 111$
$123 \times 9 + 4 = 1111$
$1234 \times 9 + 5 = 11111$
$12345 \times 9 + 6 = 111111$
$123456 \times 9 + 7 = 1111111$
$1234567 \times 9 + 8 = 11111111$
$1234568 \times 9 + 9 = 111111111$
$123456789 \times 9 + 10 = 1111111111$

$6^2 = 36$
$66^2 = 4356$
$666^2 = 443556$
$6666^2 = 44435556$
$66666^2 = 4444355556$
$666666^2 = 444443555556$
$6666666^2 = 4444443555556$

$1 \times 8 + 1 = 9$
$12 \times 8 + 2 = 98$
$123 \times 8 + 3 = 987$
$1234 \times 8 + 4 = 9876$
$12345 \times 8 + 5 = 98765$
$123456 \times 8 + 6 = 987654$
$1234567 \times 8 + 7 = 9876543$
$12345678 \times 8 + 8 = 98765432$
$123456789 \times 8 + 9 = 987654321$

$9 \times 9 + 7 = 88$
$98 \times 9 + 6 = 888$
$987 \times 9 + 5 = 8888$
$9876 \times 9 + 4 = 88888$
$98765 \times 9 + 3 = 888888$
$987654 \times 9 + 2 = 8888888$
$9876543 \times 9 + 1 = 88888888$

About the Author
Thomas Biesanz

Tom is a semi-retired teacher who taught an advanced math course. He then taught test preparation for Math and English, and saw that many students have a negative attitude about math that kept them from learning. Since he was convinced that numbers are interesting, his focus was on getting students **curious** about numbers. He had no intention of creating a math teaching system. This fun, right-brain approach is the result of working with individual students. He also has a Masters in Counseling, which helped him to be attentive to how students can change their outlook on Math.

He recently changed over to a Mac computer, and this book is better because of it. He loves dancing, especially Contra, West Coast, and the Waltz (1, 2, <u>3</u>, 1, 2, <u>3</u>...). He is also taking up surfing in his Sixties, riding a Trikke (Trikke. com) and goes whale watching regularly. His other interests are the Conscious Relationship work of Gay and Katie Hendricks and the Mankind Project that assists men in finding their mission in life.

He grew up in Minnesota and now lives in Santa Barbara, California with his wife, Jan, and two cats, where he writes, teaches, and does teacher trainings. He has 3 married children and 5 grandchildren, including Oscar, who is in kindergarden and recently made his first EZ Times Table. See Oscar on the web at http://Youtube/user/MisterNumbers

He hopes the EZ Times Table makes math less mysterious and more playful. He believes that it opens students' minds to view things from a curious point of view.

"Remember, NumbersREZ!" ("Numbers are easy!")

Dedication: to Bill Biesanz, who inspired me to be creative and Irene Biesanz who shared her love of people and learning.

Thanks to Teresa, Francis, Brian, David, Joy, Marty, Jeff, Charlotte and others who helped with their feedback. Thanks to the Santa Barbara Charter School for allowing me to use this innovative system with their students. Thanks to Jakob Marsh who did the awesome drawings on the weekend before he left for Germany for a year. Thanks to my bride Jan, who gave me support and offered this book artistic and editorial touches. Thanks to the Universe that funneled this project through me.

Website: EZTimesTable.com
Blog site: EZTimesTable/numbers
Contact Tom at eztimestable@aol.com

10 Main Benefits Showing Why EZ Times Table (EZTT), Right-brain Math, Should Be Included In K- 5ᵗʰ grade

1) EZTT **reveals** the whole **times table** from patterns while kids have **fun creating it.**

2) Students combine learning with playing with patterns **(right-brain).** They are motivated and form a **positive attitude toward math.**

3) **EZ** Times Table (EZTT**) creates a structure**, a one page graphic organizer, for understanding numbers that makes sense to kids. **Factors and squares** are immediately recognizable in EZTT.

4) EZTT appeals to a variety of students, and effective because it is based on **multiple learning strategies**.

5) **EZTT is based on the Ones and Twos**, which are easy for students. This helps them "own" multiplication because it makes sense to them.

6) **EZTT** is fundamental and can be seen as multiplication **OR repeated addition.**

7) EZTT can be used in kindergarten to teach a **number line**, in first grade to teach **addition and subtraction**. It can use the same structure to flow effortlessly into multiplication, and then to **tables, graphs, place value, factors, and prime numbers**.

8) **EZTT teaches pattern recognition** which is important in all areas of learning (right-brain).

9) **EZTT is complementary to other math teaching methods** such as arrays, object grouping, grids on graph paper, flash cards, number lines, and more.

10)   EZTT fits **kids learning style**, which is more right-brained, interested in **rhythm, patterns, sound, relationships** and looking at an **overview**.

Quick Order Form

Fax orders: **805-967-0469**

Telephone orders: **805-967-0469**

Email orders: Orders@EZTimesTable.com

Postal orders: EZ Times Table, 4025 State Street #9, Santa Barbara, CA 93110

Please send _____ copies of EZ Times Table at $12.95. Include tax in CA (7.75%) and shipping ($3 each). Total $_____

Name: _____ **Address:**_____

City: _____ **State** _____ **Zip:** _____ **email:** _____

Phone: _____ **Payment:** ☐ Check ☐ Visa ☐ Mastercard

Card Number: _____

Name on Card: _____ **Exp date:** _____